A Pilgrim's way

Also by J. Barrie Shepherd

*A Child Is Born: Meditations
for Advent and Christmas*

*Praying the Psalms: Daily Meditations
on Cherished Psalms*

*Prayers from the Mount: Daily Meditations
on the Sermon on the Mount*

*Encounters: Poetic Meditations
on the Old Testament*

*A Diary of Prayer: Daily Meditations
on the Parables of Jesus*

Diary of Daily Prayer

A Pilgrim's Way

Meditations for Lent and Easter

J. Barrie Shepherd

Westminster/John Knox Press
Louisville, Kentucky

Scripture quotations from the Revised Standard Version of the Bible are copyrighted 1946, 1952, © 1971, 1973 by the Division of Christian Education of the National Council of the Churches of Christ in the U.S.A. and are used by permission.

The meditation for Good Friday morning first appeared in print in shorter form in *alive now!* March/April '81.

Book design by Peter Gall

First edition

Published by Westminster/John Knox Press
Louisville, Kentucky

PRINTED IN THE UNITED STATES OF AMERICA
9 8 7 6 5 4 3 2 1

Library of Congress Cataloging-in-Publication Data

Shepherd, J. Barrie.
  A pilgrim's way : meditations for Lent and Easter / J. Barrie
Shepherd.—1st. ed.
      p.   cm.
  ISBN 0-664-25067-X

  1. Lent—Prayer books and devotions—English.   2. Easter—Prayer
books and devotions—English.   3. Devotional calendars.   I. Title.
BV85.S494 1989
242'.34—dc20   89-31957
                                                         CIP

I dedicate this book to Pauline Gatewood
and the staff of the Swarthmore Presbyterian Church;
and all those who have worked with me
as colleagues in ministry:

Frank Gillespie,
Bob Richardson, Peg Ferguson,
J. Harry Cotton, Karin Nelson,
Bill Henderson, Cynthia Jarvis.

"I give thanks to God always for you."

Contents

Preface

As one who has now written some seven books of prayer and meditation, I am occasionally approached as an "expert" in this particular field. However, one thing I have learned from all these endeavors is that there is no such thing as an expert in the field of prayer. This is an area in which we are all fellow students, fellow seekers; and we need to learn from one another.

If I have been given any particular gift—and Paul would have us believe that we all receive some gift from God—then mine might be that of a joy in words, an ability to put words and phrases together in ways that invite and encourage the comprehending participation of other believers. Thus it may be my privilege to unlock the door to the house of prayer. But once I have done so, you are the one who must lift the latch, push that door open, step across the threshold, and make the house your own.

As Leslie Weatherhead so helpfully pointed out in *A Private House of Prayer,* there are many chambers to this dwelling place—rooms called "Praise" and "Adoration," others called "Petition" and "Intercession," even an entrance hallway called "Confession, Repentance, and Grace." The furnishing of these rooms is up to you, the reader and prayer of this book. The framework and the unlocked door are provided within these pages; the rest is your own affair.

As a Lenten prayer diary this book is based on the Common Lectionary, which is being increasingly used by churches across the United States. I have selected the scripture passages for each day from the various options offered by the three-year cycle of the Lectionary and then sought to bring out at least a few of the insights revealed to me there. For most of the days, one lesson is chosen and then prayers for morning and evening are derived from that portion of the scriptures. It is therefore essential for understanding and participation in the prayers first to read and reflect upon the chosen passage before venturing on to the actual printed meditations. It may prove helpful to maintain, alongside this book, your personal notebook "Prayer Diary," so that, as these prayers evoke fresh insights and perceptions within yourself, they can be recorded and become the journal of your own Lenten pilgrimage.

In these expectant weeks when our northern world begins to break the hold of winter and move toward spring—these light-expanding, "lengthening" days of Lent—Christians over the centuries have found it a transforming exercise in faith and hope to return to the scriptures and retrace the path of our Lord as he steadfastly "set his face to go to Jerusalem." It is my prayer in presenting this book that through these pages your Lenten season may be enriched—your mind and spirit led along the way that passes through the wilderness, to Golgotha and the garden's empty tomb . . . and then beyond.

J.B.S.

Swarthmore, Pennsylvania
Epiphany 1989

When the days drew near for him to be received up, he set his face to go to Jerusalem.

—Luke 9:51

A Pilgrim's Way

ASH WEDNESDAY

Joel 2:12–18

MORNING

Rend your hearts and not your garments

These days we do not even rend
our garments, let alone our hearts.
Repentance seems an out-of-place,
old-fashioned concept in a world where
the word "sin" has lost all meaning,
depravity has been explained as faulty genes
or lack of proper education,
and ethics have been rendered down
to what one can or cannot get away with.

This "fasting . . . weeping . . . mourning"
that is called for would be seen by most today
as pathological behavior, a bizarre overreaction
to a momentary setback in one's self-esteem.
Even churches seem so eager to proclaim
the full assurance of God's pardon,
the wideness of the divine mercy,
to set aside all thought of judgment,
any word of guilt or holy, righteous condemnation,
that penitence would seem superfluous, no longer needed
in the free-market economy of "Amazing Grace."

On this day of ashes,
in this season set aside for honesty
and genuine, far-reaching self-examination,
speak to me, Lord God, through this your word:

speak of judgment that must come before forgiveness,
of the forthright recognition of my failure,
my futility, my emptiness, a recognition
which lays the sure and firm foundation
for repentance and new life.

Cure me from the curse
of cheap and easy grace held forth
by the religious hucksters of this age.
And lead me through the trials of the desert
to that city with the gates which open wide
to welcome all who seek your grace because
.they have none of their own.

Rend my heart today,
Lord God, then mend it by
your healing word of mercy
and of steadfast love.
                    Amen.

Joel 2:12–18

EVENING

Spare thy people, O LORD

These ashes that we wear this holy day
ground us against the earth of grim reality;
they impress upon our brows, against our minds,
the strict and severe limitation set on all we are,
all we have, all we do and hope to do.

   Remember you are dust,
   and to dust you shall return—

rich syllables which recall us to our origin,
remind us of our inevitable end,
renew for us the call to make the present count,
to "work while there is light,"
to heed the word of judgment and of hope
that is the gospel.

They set our days within a stringent context,
at once more narrow and more broad:
the narrow context of the grave,
that one sure fate that awaits all God's children,
the wide, eternal context of God's grace
set before all to choose or to refuse.

This has been a solemn day;
after Good Friday, the most solemn in the year.
I have felt the grit of ash upon my forehead,
the grit of judgment and of death upon my life.
Yet like the sand and grit we scatter
across winter-slippery roads and sidewalks,
these ashes, too, give traction, slow down
the giddy, insane slide across the weeks and months,
provide a grip, firm foothold from which to move
ahead in search of meaning, depth,
a future to hold on to.

In the days and weeks to come, Lord,
guide my footsteps to the steady places,
moments of quiet prayer and contemplation,
hours spent in study, meditation, discussion,
growth in faith and understanding, participation
in the worship of the Christian community,
action in the cause of peace and justice,
deeds of love that build the human family.

Now guard my sleep this night;
may I rest my bones within your promise
that can reach far beyond this dust and ashes
toward the shining vestments of eternity.
                                        Amen.

DAY TWO

James 1:12–18

MORNING

Let no one say . . . "I am tempted by God"

Sometimes the gospel reaches out
in surprising and even amusing ways.
I saw a T-shirt recently which bore the message:

> Lead me not into temptation,
> I can find it for myself.

and when I had done smiling I realized
just how much truth lies in that tricky slogan.

James says the same thing here when he writes:

> for God cannot be tempted with evil
> and he himself tempts no one.

Yet there is a testing God permits
the faithful to go through, a trying time
like those forty days of Jesus in the wilderness,
when Satan—or our own desires, as James here
would suggest—attempts to lure us, to entice us
into selfish actions which defy the holy will,
which would deny God's sovereign claim.

Indeed, there is no sin in being tempted;
it is the yielding to temptation that separates
and distances from God. I remember Luther's comment
that we cannot stop birds flying over our heads,
but we can prevent their nesting in our hair.

Might it even be possible
that temptations, when handled properly
and overcome, can be transformed from weakness
into areas of strength and future confidence?
As a mended limb is sometimes stronger
than before that bone was broken,
so a tested life, like steel out of the furnace,
is tempered to a new resilience, a deeper,
fuller, and more compassionate understanding.

One thing is certain:
When we are tested God does not leave,
abandon us to face that test alone.
The testimony of the saints is that, with every test,
the Lord supplies sufficient strength and power
to resist and be victorious. All I must do
is accept the help that is already there.

In every test of this new day, Lord God,
help me to see and grasp your guiding hand.

Amen.

James 1:12–18

EVENING

Every perfect gift is from above

James reminds me here,
in this shadowed evening hour,
that all light originates with God;
and God's light, unlike the everchanging,
waxing, waning rays of distant sun and moon,
is a light which never wavers, flickers, or grows **dim**.
It is the light of love, that selfsame light
John writes about as being found in Christ—
the Life of all—a light that shines in darkness
and is never overshadowed, never vanquished.

Yet in my life, even during this past day,
there have been shadows, areas of darkness
and defeat in which I have obscured the light,
set myself between its shining and the task at hand,
the neighbor in need, and, casting my own shadow,
blocked out the rays of God's bright love.
I think of all the ways in which those
"good endowments . . . perfect gifts"
have been bestowed: the comfortable home,
good food, and friendly faces which were with me,
all about me, as this day began; the tasks
which occupied my hands, my mind, my talents,
through the working hours; the colleagues and
companions who shared my day, enlivened it with laughter,
or enlarged its sense of purpose. I am mindful of
the evening hours with family, or in pursuit of
hobbies, interests, entertainment, service of
community or church. And as I pass this day
before my inner eye—shadows and sunshine—
I perceive my Lord has been beside me,
walking with me, offering at every step
bright gifts which would dispel, if I accept them,
every darkness, lead me further into light.

O God, forgive those hurtful acts,
or healing acts neglected, which have
increased darkness rather than light.
Add to your perfect gifts one further blessing:
the gift of steadfast love, enduring mercy
which will lighten every darkened place
and bear me through this night upon
the shining wings of grace.
In Christ, my Lord, I ask it.
                              Amen.

DAY THREE

Genesis 2:7–9; 3:1–7

The tree of the knowledge of good and evil

Back to the beginning again.
Before Lent can proceed very far,
it seems I must retrace my steps and look
at where it all began, that mystery portrayed
within this ancient story of a garden and a tree.

Why did God plant it in the first place?
Why did the Lord set this challenge
at the heart of our reality, this possibility,
this almost-invitation to defy the holy admonition
and to grasp after the unknown?
I have wondered, with everyone who reads this tale,
about the serpent and the role he plays.
Where did he come from? Was he part of God's creation,
included in the plan? It would seem he told the truth
about the tree and the potential of its fruit,
and yet is cursed for doing so.

Somehow I am reminded of that other one
who bore the curse, of Judas and his strangely
necessary role around that other fateful tree,
the cross at Golgotha. Without the serpent
there would have been no sin, but might there also
be no virtue? The moral choice he introduced,
that "knowledge of good and evil,"
is essential to what we call "human being."

For us to freely choose the good, for us to
"love the Lord our God," we must also have the option
of denial, the other choice of loving our own self.
And if Judas had not played his part, a part which,
even in the Gospels, seems destined, foreordained,
then the cross, the Easter tomb, the redemption
that they brought could not have happened.

This mystery of evil, Lord,
in all its singular and seeming necessity,
has been a puzzle for the most inquiring minds
that ever lived. I thank you for their legacy.
I thank you for the mystery, and pray
that in and through this rich enigma you might
bring me to sufficient truth to do the right,
to live by grace, to trust myself this day
to your creating and redeeming ways,
through Christ who lived your mystery among us
and revealed its heart as love.

> Amen.

Genesis 2:7–9; 3:1–7

EVENING

Then the eyes of both were opened

It has long intrigued me
that the very first result of sin
was the awareness of self,
self-consciousness:

> Then the eyes of both were opened,
>   and they knew that they were naked;

so that shame was the initial response;
that, and the attempt to cover up.

This relationship of self and sin
is a complex one. It seems in Genesis
as if the whole development of self, at least

as I know self today, is born from sin,
the product of rebellion against God.
And yet in teaching to love neighbor as oneself,
Jesus implied a healthy love of self as
not just permissible but necessary.

One has to have a self,
even to cherish self as God's good gift,
in order to be able to give that self away,
to lose, then find it once again, as Jesus taught.
There has to be a difference
between being—even loving—oneself
and selfishness: the choice of oneself over God,
which is the very basis for all sin.

There must have been in that old story
a sense in which Adam and Eve were selves,
already knew themselves as whole and separate beings,
before their eyes were opened to themselves
as naked and ashamed.

Guide me to know, Lord God,
that genuine and honest self-regard
which values self as part of your creation
and for all that it can be and bring and give
to a world in need of such gifts as you have
entrusted to my care. But preserve me
from the self-centered existence
that only heeds your voice when it commands
what I would want to do in any case,
and otherwise ignores your call
to freely set myself beneath your will,
your wisdom for my days.
                    Amen.

DAY FOUR

1 Corinthians 9:19–27

MORNING

Free from all . . . a slave to all

As I encounter once again
this man Paul and his writings,
I am grateful for his flair, his enthusiasm,
his masterful presentation of the faith which—
even across the chasm of two thousand years,
an ancient language—still resonates with power.

Paul speaks here with the passion,
the devotion of a lover as he presents—
in this great discussion of Christian freedom—
the way he views his freedom from the law.
He affirms his liberty in ringing terms:

Am I not free? Am I not an apostle?
Have I not seen Jesus our Lord?

And yet he joyously subjects that liberty,
is even ready to sacrifice it when necessary,
to the greater joy he knows in the gospel.

Paul is willing to accept the law
or to be free of it, to show weakness
or true strength, to know poverty, hunger,
imprisonment, even death,
for the sake of the love he has found,
the acceptance he has known,
the hope he has been given in Christ.

I do it all for the sake of the gospel,
that I may share in its blessings.

In practical terms this means Paul places
his whole life and every detail of it in God's hands,
at the Lord's disposal. Out of genuine concern
for fellow men and women, he is willing to give up
whatever it will take to lead them to the Master.

Such passion and devotion, Lord,
fill me with wonder and, at the same time,
sadness at the dimensions of my own poor dedication.
In face of Paul's joyful abandon
I find myself so often grudging, calculating even,
in my own discipleship.

Help me to learn from Paul,
to catch from him, not any spirit
of grim and dutiful self-sacrifice;
rather, his experience of overwhelming,
liberating joy.
                    Amen.

1 Corinthians 9:19–27

EVENING

Self-control in all things

Paul's image here of runners in a race
is certainly familiar; people are running,
jogging, exercising self-control,
pommeling their bodies in all sorts of ways
in this fitness-oriented world.
There is something almost puritanical—
the absolute devotion of the true believer—
about the way folk work, eat, study,
even debate nowadays to drive their bodies
as close to perfection as is possible,
given the harsh realities of time and tide.

I myself am part of this whole movement,
and I find, through moderate, regular exercise,
that mind and even spirit can be helped
by such a discipline. Nevertheless,
I cannot but observe that for true devotees,
those who spend hours of each day
in various severe regimens of super-fitness,
the whole thing can take on aspects of religion,
a searching for salvation, the quest,
if not for eternity, at least to stave off
old mortality for as long as is physically possible.

Athletics here, for Paul, are presented
not for themselves but as a metaphor,
an image of the spiritual life.
He urges me to emulate the boxer or the runner
in a footrace, but to imitate their attitudes,
not their actions. It is the discipline,
the strict self-control, that Paul claims
for himself, not the athletic prowess.

For all my constant struggles with diet and weight,
as one example, I suspect I sometimes wrestle
harder there than I do in daily prayer.
But then, the results, or lack of same,
are so much more clearly evident
in the physical realm than with the spirit.

Help me bring to all my prayers
and—beyond prayer—to my daily living of the faith,
the determination and endurance of the athlete.
That when this race is ended I may, by grace,
be fit to wear the victor's crown.
                              Amen.

DAY FIVE

Deuteronomy 26:5–11

MORNING

And you shall make response before the LORD

The people, Israel, said these words
when they came before the Lord to remember
all God's blessings and give thanks.
They recited their own history,
going back to Abram, that "wandering Aramean,"
and then moving through captivity and oppression
to deliverance, exodus and promised land—
that place of milk and honcy.
Then they took the firstfruits, finest samples of
their harvest, and returned them gratefully,
in recognition of the divine goodness and mercy.

Memory was such a vibrant, living thing
to those ancient Israelites. No mere nostalgia,
no longing for good old days that never really were;
it was rather an activity that set the present
in its place, even shaped the future.
In memory the Hebrew people saw their own foundations.
They looked back and traced God's hand in all
that happened to them, joys and tribulations,
their journeyings and coming home.
They drew lessons from the past,
recognized those principles which led them
to prosperity or which, neglected, brought them
to the brink of desolation and despair.
And then, in light of what had been,

they turned to face the future with new insight
and new confidence, assured that, if they only
kept those laws, acknowledged their own Lord,
they would prosper in the place
God had given them to live.

As I look across my days and years this Sunday morning,
I too can see your presence, Lord, can recognize,
in ways that were not possible back then,
just how you guided me and led me to this moment,
this stage in life, this complex interaction
of fear and hope, problem and opportunity,
which forms, for me, the present.

Continue with me through this Sabbath day
and every day that lies ahead
until I reach your promised land
and offer there the full fruits of my days
in grateful praise.
                    Amen.

Deuteronomy 26:5–11

EVENING

You shall rejoice

Rejoicing has long been a problem
for Christians of the mainstream variety.
Ask us to educate, legislate, officiate,
even to ameliorate, and we respond quite well;
but rejoicing doesn't seem to be our thing.
Add to all this the reality of Lent—and the call
in today's lesson to rejoice seems out of place.

On the other hand, wherever one looks in the Bible
one finds this selfsame summons. The psalms,
for all their heavy treatment of depravity and despair,
continually break out in peals of irrepressible gladness;

while Paul, in the midst of all his trials and tribulations,
can urge his fellow Christians to

> Rejoice in the Lord always;
> again I will say, Rejoice.

Jesus was accused because he refused to suppress
his clear delight in the people and things of creation.
He set his life against all who turned religion
into a list of crushing duties, obligations,
rules that squeezed the juice from life
like a steamroller crushing an orange.
Why has Christ's church since then
deserted the poor orange
and hopped aboard the steamroller?

Perhaps the problem lies in how people
understand this "joy." It is no empty optimism,
the attempt to evade harsh reality
by wearing a happy face.
Jesus and the psalmists found their joy
not in shutting out the problems of the world,
but at the very heart of reality's hurt and turmoil.
And Francis, Luther, Mother Teresa, Martin Luther King,
shared a joy that plumbs the depth of pain and yet
can wear a smile forever true and undefeated.
No empty laughter theirs, but honest recognition—
with fully open eyes—of the loveliness deep hidden
in each life, each corner of this globe.
And only eyes of faith, it seems, can pierce beyond
to open up creation's vast neglected reservoirs
of flowing, genuine joy.

Teach me, O God, to see myself, my neighbor,
and my world in such a truly joyful way.

Amen.

DAY SIX

Matthew 4:1–11

MORNING

To be tempted

Jesus, in this wilderness confrontation,
is offered several methods, alternative approaches,
as it were, to winning people to his side.

The first temptation comes through his own hunger.
But might this also be a way to reach the hungry crowd?
Transforming stones into bread—in that day
or this—will swiftly bring an empire to one's feet.
Or again, the temptation to test God's power
by leaping from the temple pinnacle
could also be a way of attracting attention,
popular support, through miraculous deeds.

Neither of these acts, in and of themselves,
appears particularly sinful or depraved.
They could reasonably be called "in a good cause";
certainly not the kind of scandalous,
flagrantly heinous sins one might imagine
his satanic majesty dealing in.
Yet, just because this is so,
these temptations are particularly dangerous.
These acts involve perversions of the good,
the twisting and manipulation of divine power
to serve unworthy, selfish ends.
So that despite innocuous appearance,
such acts would sow corruption at the heart

of Jesus' nature, invalidate his mission
before it is properly begun.

In this wilderness of Lent I sense
temptations not unlike those Jesus met.
The tendency to glory in the trappings of the season;
to lose oneself in ritual, in color and in custom,
and neglect the penitence the prophets spoke of,
a penitence displayed in acts of justice,
deeds of genuine love and mercy.
There is peril, in this time of self-examination,
in becoming so obsessed with searching out one's sins
that one fails to recognize the powers for good
that God has set within the soul, and sinks
into an apathetic trough of condemnation and despair.

Guard me, Lord, from perversions of the good.
Grant the guidance and discernment of your Spirit,
in this and every hour of trial and testing.
Amen.

Matthew 4:1–11

Fall down and worship me

The tempter finally reveals himself
in this third and last temptation,
offering everything, every *thing* conceivable,
if Jesus only renders him obeisance.
And here we see the basic nature of all sin.
Sin does not consist so much in acts,
forbidden in some arbitrary way;
sin is centered in the question of allegiance,
of what or whom I live my life toward.

To worship Satan means to grant him worth,
to make him worthy, worthy of praise and adoration,
the service of my mind, my strength, my soul.

In return the tempter offers much,
much that my distracted self cherishes greatly:

    All the kingdoms of the world
    and the glory of them.

Jesus had come to save the world; and here,
at the outset, that world is offered on a silver platter.

I will never face temptation on such a scale.
The kingdoms of this world are rarely offered to
the average believer. On the other hand
there is a sense in which, whenever I must choose
between success bought at the price of compromise
and seeming failure with integrity intact,
I face the same dilemma Jesus faced.

One can choose the kingdoms of the world
by using the convenient lie,
the almost necessary evasion of the truth.
Many actions, or inactions, may be elegantly
rationalized in the name of service to the church
or future benefits that far outweigh a momentary
lapse in love, concern, or Christian charity.
It is so easy to believe that one can play the game
for now—using rules the world lays down—
then renounce the whole thing at a later,
safer, more expedient date.

O God, fix my gaze firm on you this night,
on the challenge and the promise, the great offer
of allegiance set before me in Jesus Christ my Lord.
Thus fit me for your kingdom and your glory,
a glory that will never pass away.
                          Amen.

DAY SEVEN

Genesis 15:1–6

MORNING

O Lord GOD, what wilt thou give me?

"Fear not" and other sweeping generalities
are all very well, but Abram requests a more
specific reassurance. His is a practical concern.
He wants to know just what the Lord his God has done
for him lately. What good, in other words, are promises
when he is still without an heir, and all he owns
will be passed down to Eliezer, his manservant?

That's the trouble with the promises of scripture.
They will persist in speaking to the cosmic questions,
when what I need to know is how to pay the bills,
what to tell my boss, an instant cure for cancer,
and the quickest way to put a broken family back together.

Details give the shape to my most urgent problems,
those everyday concerns with not the slightest impact
on the future of the cosmos, yet they make my life
a heaven or a hell. I realize that, ultimately,
it could make all the difference to know God
is in control, to rest in the assurance
that my destiny is held in divine hands.
But ultimate concerns and eventual destinies
are not the stuff of daily, hourly crisis;
and before I can consider them I need to make it
through the next disaster coming down the pike.

These characters in the scriptures
knew their share and more of crisis and disaster.
From what I read they seemed to fail at least
as often as they triumphed, and their faith
in God was not exactly steadfast and unshaken.
What is amazing is the faith God placed in them:
that patient and persistent trust that,
in the end, they would hold firm;
the commitment of all plans,
hopes, and dreams for future generations
into those faltering, wavering, shaky,
even shifty human lives.

Might there even be a part for me
in your design, Lord God?
If so, then may I play it with all the life
you have given me. Despite my fearful lack of faith,
let your great faith in me be vindicated,
through Christ my Lord.
                              Amen.

Genesis 15:1–6

EVENING

Look toward heaven, and number the stars

August nights in Maine
I wander out to the bluff in front
of our island cottage just before bedtime
and gaze into the starlit sky. So much more
is to be seen out there, far away from the blazing
glare of the glittering East Coast megalopolis.

Words from Shakespeare, memorized in high school—
about a hundred years ago, it seems—come to mind:

  Look how the floor of heaven
  Is thick inlaid with patines of bright gold.
  There's not the smallest orb which thou behold'st

But in his motion like an angel sings,
Still quiring to the young-ey'd cherubins;
Such harmony is in immortal souls;
But whilst this muddy vesture of decay
Doth grossly close it in, we cannot hear it.

Sometimes, out there beneath the stars,
I can almost hear that harmony Shakespeare wrote of.
Other times I stare into the magnitudes of space
and I feel dwarfed, completely insignificant—
a momentary blip, on a microscopic dot,
in a corner of an unimportant galaxy.

For Abram the stars became a metaphor
to illustrate God's covenant, assurance of posterity—
an innumerable multitude to carry on the promise.
Abram accepted that assurance, and his trust
became what is called "righteousness."

Lord, even as I pray to you tonight,
the stars stretch out their canopy of light,
your panoply of promise, far above my head.
Drive out the timid, fearful ways that I respond
at times to all the wonder of your universe.
Teach me to forget about myself—
my significance or insignificance
in face of the vast cosmos.
Grant me instead to know that faith
by which I can lose myself in contemplation
of the beauty, the glory, the grandeur,
and the majesty of your design.
Then assure me that I have my part,
my role to play, my destiny within
that sweeping, radiant grandeur
that sings of light, of loveliness,
of grace, of hope, of love.
                    Amen.

DAY EIGHT

Romans 10:8–13

MORNING

The word of faith which we preach

That righteousness I read about in Genesis
last night, Abram's righteousness of trust,
of confidence in God's assurances,
is renewed here by Paul as he wrestles
with the question of salvation.

Over against the elaborate arrangements
of the religious experts, the rituals and dogmas,
prescriptions and proscriptions, put forward as
the one and only way to gain God's favor;
over against the ten-point plans and schemes,
those emotional TV appeals, checks in the mail,
the "fire escapes" of the superrich,
the piling up of prayers and candles,
good deeds based in guilt rather than compassion;
over against every human attempt to win, to earn,
to merit or deserve God's grace
this word of Paul calls simply for belief.

Salvation, which means life, whole life,
healed life, abundant, rich, and never-ending life,
cannot be purchased, earned, or worked toward;
it is available exclusively and freely as a gift.
And all this gift requires is that I live it
and I "be" it—in other words, "be-li(e)ve" it—
live it out with every moment of my freely gifted being.

But that living-out has shape to it and form.
It bears the faithful outline of those who walked
this way before: yes, Abraham and Paul;
above all, that One in whom the gift of life in trust
was finally and winningly set down upon this earth.
He showed it to be full of grace and truth,
of hope, concern for others, understanding
and compassion for our human plight,
of self-forgetful love which bore the weight
of all our need and hungers, fear and shameful failures,
even hate and blind hostility to show the height
and depth of the divine trustworthiness.

As I step out into this day,
in every moment, everything I do and say,
let me show forth, great God, that trust
which saves my life for life,
for life in faith in you.

                              Amen

Romans 10:8–13

EVENING

The word is near you, on your lips and in your heart

Paul speaks, in these encouraging words,
of the naturalness of faith. He sees that trust
in God is not some odd and almost overwhelming challenge,
a goal requiring massive moral or intellectual effort,
but is more like breathing in and breathing out.
He quotes Moses here, who used these selfsame words—
this image of intimacy and closeness—
in Moab, on the very borders of the promised land,
to call Israel to faith before she entered in
to claim her ancient promises. He urged the people
to look back, remember their deliverance, the mercies
that accompanied them in the wilderness, and thus
to realize that life for them, identity, and hope

were all bound up in their relationship,
their fidelity to God.

As I look back across the days and years,
as I review my journey—the wildernesses and
the lovely, fertile places—I discover once again
the truth and wonder Paul and Moses spoke of.
I realize that God has always been there,

> closer than breathing,
> nearer than hands and feet,

and that my strenuous efforts,
all those prodigous undertakings, have not been
to believe, but rather to avoid belief.

How natural a thing it is, really,
to acknowledge my dependence, my awe
before God's majesty, my need before God's mercy,
my life within God's presence and God's providence.
As natural as the infant's hand that reaches out
and grasps for something, someone to hold on to,
is this urge to set my hand, my self, my destiny
within the strong, providing context of God's grace.
I was created, my body, mind, and spirit
were designed for life like this.
And yet I do not live it, but choose
instead the self-defeating ways of fear, mistrust,
reliance on my own attempts to run my life, save myself.

Forgive my blindness, O my God, my failure
to accept this truth that stares me in the face.
Envelop me within your grace, and fold me
in your everlasting arms this night.
Amen.

DAY NINE

Isaiah 58:3–12

MORNING

The fast that I choose

The spiritual discipline of fasting,
so much a part of Lent in years gone by,
seems, nowadays, a long-outdated undertaking,
something almost medieval in its connotations,
akin to mortification, flagellation, and the like.
And yet for completely other reasons,
in particular the loss of excess weight,
people, it seems, are fasting more than ever.

Israel's prophets were not impressed by fasting,
for whatever reason. They were quick to perceive,
as Isaiah puts it:

> Behold, in the day of your fast
> you seek your own pleasure.

They saw, as Jesus did, that the fasting of their day
was all too often an attempt to impress others
with their own displays of piety
or to manipulate and seek to win God's favor.

The prophets spoke repeatedly
of the urgent need to undergird the fasting
and other practices and rituals of their time
with that far more difficult spiritual discipline,
obedience to the holy laws of God.
They saw the blasphemy in artificial hunger,

in the momentary, voluntary experience of starvation
by those who might have all the food they wished
if they so ordered, when, at the same time,
often in the same city, orphans and widows
had no other option but to starve.

They called, in the Lord's name,
for a fast that would wipe out hunger,
not mimic it; for a humility that could stoop
low enough to see the desperation of
fellow human beings and then
do something about it.

In this season of spiritual discipline, Lord God,
let me not neglect the traditional disciplines—
prayer, meditation, even a proper fasting—
but beyond all these, guide me toward
that discipline on which all others stand,
the discipline of Christian charity
in all I do, to all I meet.
                                        Amen.

Isaiah 58:3–12

EVENING

The repairer of the breach

These scriptures are full of titles.
There are, for one thing, many names for God,
descriptive phrases by which we catch a glimpse
of what and who the Lord is: "Rock and Redeemer,"
"Shepherd of Israel," "the Holy One."
There are also lofty names and honorifics
for those who lead the nation as kings and queens,
judges, priests, generals, and the like.
Of all these titles, one that has long intrigued,
one that, perhaps, appeals to me the most,
is contained in this promise from Isaiah:

You shall be called the repairer of the breach,
the restorer of streets to dwell in.

So many folk are swift to tear things down.
This world has never lacked for demolition experts,
those who excel in breaking apart, in creating a breach,
in the calculating skills of destruction, devastation,
techniques of creating division, fostering hostility.

For my own self, I confess that it seems
so much easier and self-satisfying to take offense,
even to pick a quarrel, rather than to seek out
reconciliation, to work with care and tenderness,
painstaking skill toward the mending of divisions,
the healing of broken relationships,
the binding up of wounds.

As I confess my failure in this regard,
I remember and give thanks for Jesus Christ
who repaired, once for all, the gaping breach
that separated me from all that is holy and good,
who built a bridge with his own body between my failure
and God's mercy, between my need and the divine abundance.

I give thanks also this night for all
who carry out the quiet, world-transforming task
of reconciliation in these hostile, fearful times;
for dedicated teachers, social workers, honest judges,
and those who govern well, for peacekeepers
of all kinds and parents too and faithful friends.
Teach me, Lord, to set myself among that fellowship.
Grant that someday I also may be called

a repairer of the breach,
a restorer of streets to dwell in.

Amen.

DAY TEN

1 Peter 3:18–22

MORNING

He preached to the spirits in prison

This fascinating image of Jesus
preaching to the lost souls in hell,
offering his gospel to those who lived
before his incarnation, was devised
by early Christian preachers as an answer
for two important questions. First:
What was Jesus doing in the time that passed
between his crucifixion and resurrection?
And second: What about the fate of all
those persons born in centuries past who never
had their chance to hear the gospel and believe?

These questions, especially the second,
trouble many Christians to this day.
The concept of an actual hell where people—
even those who never heard the saving word of life—
suffer torment and are punished for eternity
is not merely troubling or frightening;
it seems to contradict the very basis of the gospel,
that love for neighbor which was taught
and lived out by the Christ himself.

If God is the kind of deity Jesus spoke about
and demonstrated by his life and ministry, the kind
of heavenly Father I can address in prayer
and simple trust, then that vast and infinite love

must be inconceivably more devastated than mine
by the prospect of its own beloved creatures
undergoing everlasting pain without hope
or possibility of eventual release.

I am intrigued by this concept in First Peter
of Jesus coming from the cross to harrow hell
by offering deliverance to the captives.
I am even more intrigued by suggestions
in the scriptures that God's grace and mercy
far outweigh divine anger, that God's plan
is for salvation to every human soul,
that the Lord pursues down all the corridors
of time and even of eternity till grace must triumph,
sin and pride must yield, and the whole family
is welcomed home around the festive table.

Continue, Lord, in this new day to struggle with me,
for me; and win me for your everlasting kingdom.

Amen.

1 Peter 3:18–22

EVENING

Baptism . . . now saves you

In the earliest days of the faith,
when the infant church was struggling for life
in the midst of a hostile, pagan world,
baptism must have been a much more tremendous
and even traumatic experience.
To undergo this sacrament entailed at the very least
a complete transformation, and it might well cost
the new believer's life. It was seen, therefore,
as something of great, even eternal value:
well worth the dreadful risks that it entailed.

Still today, in certain areas of the globe,
baptism—the public claiming of the Christian faith—

is a costly, risky business. But for me,
and for the church and the society I belong to,
the opposite is almost true, and not to be baptized,
not to claim the name of Christ, can create problems,
can be at least a minor disadvantage.

What does it mean to me,
this sacred act of water and the Spirit?
Certainly there can be no magic involved;
baptism is not some kind of spell in which the
pronouncing of certain words, the use of ancient signs
and symbols, transforms me from a condemned sinner
to a holy saint. I think about my baptism as
the public recognition and affirmation—
in my case by my parents and their church—
of a reality already active in my life, whether I,
or they, chose to acknowledge it or not.
That reality is God's saving grace for me
and for all persons, a grace that promises good,
that holds up a destiny of everlasting life,
and that will support me, contend with me,
rebuke me, judge me, forgive and heal, nurture
and strengthen me, and lead me in the ways
of life if I will only follow.

My baptism was the moment in which
I was publicly launched out upon this pilgrimage,
this pilgrimage I still pursue tonight, Lord God.
Instill in me renewed appreciation of its cost,
its call, its Christ who is my hope
at your right hand,

    with angels, authorities, and powers
    subject to him.

        Amen.

DAY ELEVEN

Psalm 91:9–16

MORNING

No evil shall befall you

But evil *does* befall me.
In my own case nothing major—as yet—
the minor slings and arrows of the average life:
disappointments in love, frustrations at work,
aggravations with family, friends, and neighbors,
fears about health and financial security.

This psalmist sings of deliverance from terror,
pestilence, and destruction, but all around I see
people who, to all outward appearances, lead decent,
upright lives yet are struck down by cancer,
AIDS, the many random forms that violence takes
within this troubled society, those routine tragedies
that make up the daily news.
In particular the suffering of children seems hard
to reconcile with the promises held out in the psalm.
There is evil, misfortune, dumb luck,
even sheer malevolence in this God-created world;
and it seems to happen without design or plan,
to be no respecter of persons.

Of course, when I consider more deeply,
I have to admit much of the suffering I see
can be directly traced to human agencies;
ambition and greed, stupidity, fear, and neglect
are responsible for far more of our problems

than we human creatures like to admit.
It lies within our power to alleviate
a great deal of humanity's pain, but we choose,
instead, to devote scarce resources to other,
more immediate and selfish goals.

And as I look within I find the roots
of at least a portion of this world's problems
within the human heart; its conflicts, lusts, desires,
the way I seek to gain the blessing yet fail to do
God's will, to bring blessing upon others.
This problem of evil and its origins seems insoluble.
One thing I can do: I can begin to deal with
the evil that lies in my own self, my own life.

Help me to see, Lord God, where I contribute to
the hurt and the injustice of this world;
then grant me strength to turn my evil
into good, through Christ my Lord.
Amen.

Psalm 91:9–16

EVENING

I will be with him in trouble

This statement toward the end
of this resounding psalm is, for me,
a more accurate and true-to-life reflection
of the Lord's protection against evil
than the words I looked at this morning.
In these verses the psalmist
does not suggest that trouble never comes
to the person who has faith. The promise is,
When trouble comes—as come it will in this world
of light and shade—God will be with me in
and through and far beyond that trouble.

Dramatic rescues—Red Sea crossings,
lions' dens, and the like—have proved to be
the exception rather than the rule in the history
of faith. The experience of most Christians
undergoing every kind of trial has not been one
of immediate and spectacular deliverance,
but rather of an abiding, steadfast presence
in the midst of trial and torment,
a presence which has made the torment bearable,
which has provided sufficient strength—
barely sufficient, it has seemed, much of the time—
yet strength and faith to bring such persons
through the darkest valley, if not in triumph
yet still surviving, and with a deeper,
truer knowledge of divine grace.

I have known such times in my own pilgrimage,
even times when I have felt myself alone, abandoned
with urgent prayers unheard, at least unanswered.
Yet looking back again from sunlight, on the other side
of shadow, I have recognized the rod and staff,
God's guidance and firm shepherding.

Help me to learn from these moments,
O my God, so that when next I feel deserted,
lost on a lonely, chill, and distant mountainside,
I might have confidence in you,
I might be wise enough to look beyond
my unreliable emotions, and in the gloom
might hear the shepherd's seeking call,
might recognize your voice of warm compassion,
and reaching out might set my hand in yours
so you can lead me home rejoicing.
Amen.

DAY TWELVE

Matthew 17:1–9

MORNING

And after six days

On this seventh day—
this Sabbath morning—I arise
and set my mind toward the mountaintop
where I will seek encounter with my God.

The worship of the faithful community
has become, for me, more than just a duty
or a habit, more than a way of meeting friends
or of seeking to ensure my eternal well-being;
it has become a need, a genuine necessity.

Deprived of this experience,
my life grows more and more shut in,
hemmed about by the frustrations,
the shortsighted ambitions of the everyday.
I find myself caught up in schemes not worthy
of my time or my devotion, beset by fears or lusts
which drag me down toward the empty round of
living this, my only chance at life, on the basis
of the seeking out of every pleasure possible
and the avoidance of all pain.

But as I seek the mountaintop,
as I join myself with others, week by week,
to grasp the majesty and wonder of true holiness;
to join my voice with others in the harmonies

of praise and prayer; to freely, fully admit
the failures of these days just passed;
to seek out and to receive a grace
that heals, renews, restores;
to hear a word that calls me
to a wider universe, a fuller time,
a family without limits and a self which knows
a destiny beyond the turning of the years;
I experience my own transfiguration,
clothing my life again in the rich
and radiant garments of eternity.

Lord, I thank you for granting me
this moment in, yet beyond time we call worship.
May I always sense its privilege and wonder.
Let me never neglect the strength
and the perspective that it brings.
Teach me, in all I do this day,
to remember your Sabbath day and keep it holy.

Amen.

Matthew 17:1–9

EVENING

They saw no one but Jesus only

As this day draws to a close,
as its rich tapestry of worship,
recreation, relaxation, fellowship, service
fades before my weary eyes, I savor this old tale
again of presence and of revelation. What can it mean?
Its images, possibilities are so many, so varied.

I am reminded tonight of the psalm I studied yesterday,
the realization that the God I meet on the mountaintop
is also One who rescues me on the windy mountainside.
These hills and mountains, rugged valleys,
so prevalent in scripture call up fond images
of my Scottish boyhood home where the bens, lochs,

wide sweeping glens conspire to bring a grandeur
to the eye, a peaceful beauty to the heart that speaks,
calls out God's name to all who listen carefully.

Yet I am most intrigued tonight by these final words
where—as the heavenly vision fades—the disciples'
eyes are filled with the vision of the Master.

What a way to go back down the mountain
and take up the tasks and trials of the plain below!
Whatever lay ahead, whatever doubts they may have known,
fears about leaving so much behind, worries about
what was to happen when they reached Jerusalem,
one thing they now knew:

> This is my beloved Son,
> with whom I am well pleased;
> listen to him.

one person they now saw:

> And when they lifted up their eyes,
> they saw no one but Jesus only.

And in that knowledge and that vision
they went forth to find their own transfiguration.

What a way for me too, Lord God,
to go back from all that this Sabbath has held
into the new week which lies ahead, seeing in the sights
and visions that surround—temptations, challenges,
calls to love and faithfulness—the face of Christ,
his joy, his gentleness, his grace!
What a way to go into this night of rest
and sleep before me now, secure in the faith,
at rest in the arms of One who sacrificed
his radiant glory that I might live and know
the joy that comes from serving you!

Amen.

DAY THIRTEEN

Genesis 12:1–7

MORNING

Go from your country and your kindred

To some extent this going forth
is the narrative of every human life.
The process of growing up is one of growing out—
of growing out of clothes and shoes and habits,
attitudes, relationships, and into more mature ones.
And in growing out we also grow beyond the home,
the family, the dependency that is so vital
to survival in the earliest years.

This can be a painful process
and there is usually risk involved,
yet each person must go through it
or fail to reach the fullness of human life
as it was created for us.

In one sense, then, we are all like Abram,
venturing forth to find a land we can call our own.
Yet folk undertake this quest for various reasons
and with different hopes and dreads.
Abram, of course, went out in faith, in obedience
to divine command. He relied upon the promise—
a great nation to be born from him—and that
he would bring blessing to the world.

Most of the rest of us have no such clear,
compelling reasons. We move out because we have to,

because the former ways are no longer wide enough,
because we want something we cannot reach
from where we stand right now.

This independence we grow into is a good thing,
I realize, and yet, following Abram, we need
to seek our independence in dependence;
dependence on the Lord and on God's goals,
and guiding destiny for our lives.

I need to learn to place my future
in your hands, Lord God, to hold the plans
I make against your eternal purpose for my days,
and to make sure the two are moving
in the same direction.

As I set out on this new week, make clear to me
your will and your design for these hours.
Then lead me forth in dependence on your grace.

Amen.

Genesis 12:1–7

EVENING

So that you will be a blessing

To become a blessing, to leave
this world a little better than I found it,
to "help somebody as I go my way": this is surely
the finest dream of many, if not most people.
What doctor has not dreamed of discovering
the cure for cancer? What farmer or food scientist
has not fantasized a miracle crop to feed
the starving nations? Even some of the most cruel
tyrants set out, in the beginning, to help people,
to seek a solution for a crisis of their time.

Yet in the end, so many fail,
so many human lives amount to, if not a curse,

at least a zero in the total welfare of our race.
Perhaps part of the problem lies in how people
conceive this goal, never growing up beyond
those adolescent dreams of world salvation,
looking to make a major contribution, to be hailed
as benefactor, Nobel Prize winner, or something on
that order; and when that does not come about,
when the years slip past and "averageness" sets in,
then the dream is set aside and lesser,
more selfish goals take over in its place.

To be a blessing lies within the reach
of every child of God. Each one has talents,
skills, and insights, and above all love to give,
which, dedicated to the common good, will leave
this world the richer for our being here.
A good parent is a blessing, as is a faithful spouse.
A fine teacher, sanitation worker, bus driver,
musician, or retired volunteer can touch other lives
with laughter or with courtesy and consideration.

I look at my own life, my work, my play,
the relationships I cherish, those I put up with,
and I ask myself what blessings I might share.
Help me to focus more on other persons' needs
and less upon my own, O God. Help me to learn again
that lesson taught us by your Son so long ago
that you have made us all in such a way
that we find joy in one another, that we know peace
in sharing it with those about us, that we grasp
life in the very act of giving it away.
Teach me to bless myself in blessing others, Lord.

Amen.

DAY FOURTEEN

Philippians 3:17–4:1

MORNING

As you have an example in us

Examples can be crucial factors
in guiding the way people live their lives.
Nowadays we call them "role models"
and talk of their importance to the young.
But examples—heroes and heroines—
are a part of life at any age.
That is at least a part of the secret of good books
and even television; they present to us alternatives—
good and evil, innocent and street-smart, clumsy
and sophisticated—alternatives from which
to choose the models we would emulate.

By modern standards of propriety
it seems arrogant of Paul to set himself up
in this text as an example to the faithful at Philippi:

> Brethren, join in imitating me.

Yet Paul was simply recognizing here a vital role
for every teacher, one that, it seems to me,
is best acknowledged rather than neglected
in any excess of false modesty.
In fact, earlier in this same epistle,
Paul holds up before his readers the one
and only true and full example for our human life
when he writes in chapter two:

Have this mind among yourselves, which you have in Christ Jesus, who, though he was in the form of God, did not count equality with God a thing to be grasped, but emptied himself, taking the form of a servant.

In my work and play this day
I will be confronted by many who would
claim me for their follower—politicians,
athletes, even actors in commercials on TV—
individuals who will tell me "Be like me" and seek
to influence things I buy, the way I vote, even my hopes
and aspirations, in ways that are to their advantage.
Some of them will be worthy of my attention;
many of them will not.

Keep me, Lord, from foolish, even sinful idolatry.
Teach me to hold all such claims up against the One
who came to demonstrate the way to life,
to check their lives against the pattern of his days,
his ways, his teachings. Mold and shape my actions
and my attitudes according to the outlines
of your will, that the risen Christ might live in me
and thus fit me for your service.

Amen.

Philippians 3:17–4:1

EVENING

Who will change our lowly body

This whole idea of resurrection
and a resurrection body seems quite alien
to modern ways of thinking.
Speculation about life after death nowadays
centers around a concept of disembodied spirits,
so that any idea of bodily resurrection seems bizarre
and is relegated to the realm of voodoo,
zombies, and Class B horror movies.

Yet Paul, for one, is quite insistent
that our present lowly bodies will be changed

into the likeness of Christ's "glorious body."
And certainly the Gospel resurrection narratives
portray a most corporeal state of being for our Lord
in which he eats meals with his friends
and may be touched and handled.

I wonder how much of the current attitude
is due to a basic prejudice against the physical.
I remember reading that the ancient Greeks,
for all their spectacular statuary,
their physical and athletic prowess,
regarded all material things as basically inferior
to the pure and eternal realms of the spirit.
Might some of our present obsession with leanness
and super-fitness find roots in attitudes like these?

The writers of the Bible view the body
with a fundamental reverence as God's creation,
and as the temple for the spirit.
Their view of the hereafter,
the heavenly kingdom or the Second Coming,
seems unabashedly physical, with cities, rivers,
mountains, trees, and bodies to enjoy them.

All of this suggests to me
that there is much that still must be revealed,
and that whatever preconceptions I now hold
will probably be set upon their head.

Deliver me, O God, from foolish speculation
concerning what lies ahead. Sustain my faith that
in the future, as in the past, I will be with you,
and that you have prepared for all your children
unimaginable blessings and wonderful surprises.

Amen.

DAY FIFTEEN

Psalm 127

MORNING

Unless the LORD builds the house

People who build something nowadays—
a house, a bridge, a business—take all kinds
of precautions before they begin, seeking to ensure
their success. They check on funding and foundations,
insurance and other forms of protection; they carry
out surveys, environmental impact studies;
some people even check out their horoscope
or consult their favorite astrologer;
but I wonder how many ask the question
the psalmist raises here, the question as to
whether the Lord will have a part in their project.

I guess to many, perhaps most builders,
that question would seem irrelevant, and yet
if their building, whatever it may be,
cannot stand up to holy scrutiny, could not welcome
divine participation, then, as the writer says,
it is in vain, an empty, worthless nothing.

People begin to build families this way.
They plan their weddings carefully, worrying
about caterers, dance bands, photographers, invitations,
flowers, honeymoon plans. They may even talk finances,
draw up contracts, plan their children in advance.
But do they invite the Lord into their programs?

Do they leave room for divine destiny
to guide and shape their days?

So much of what we plan and do is vanity,
sheer waste of time and effort and of no earthly
benefit to anyone whatever, not even our own selves,
because we neglect to consult God's planning first,
because we think that life revolves around
our needs, our hopes, our projections
and anxieties; when all the time life is a gift
disclosed within God's holy, gracious will.

As I approach the building
of this day that lies ahead, as I
make my plans and schedules for its hours,
stand by my side, great Master Builder, and place
my every effort within the overarching context
of your purpose, your design for this creation.
Set me to the building of your kingdom, Lord,
and may my labor never be in vain.

Amen.

Psalm 127

EVENING

Lo, sons are a heritage from the LORD

As the father of four daughters,
passages like this have long troubled me.
I realize, of course, that these scriptures
are a product of their own time and place,
as well as God's word for every time and place;
and yet it troubles me, and others like me,
to find such passages in our Holy Book.

One way around this problem would be
simply to read "children" where the psalmist
writes "sons"; but this avoids the issue, does not

face the harsh reality of the patriarchal society
in which these words took shape, a society in which
women not only were seen as inferior but were treated
as the private property of fathers, husbands,
rulers, lovers—all the masculine hierarchy.

I cannot believe this is or ever was God's will.
The God who delivered his people from captivity;
the God who raised up Miriam, Deborah, Jael, and Esther;
the God who worked through Sara, Rachel, Rebecca,
Tamar, Hannah, Mary, Dorcas, and the rest
is not a God who will permit one half of his creation
to be deprived of full humanity.

Indeed, even as I write these words,
and use the pronoun "his" of God,
I am conscious of the problems this use raises,
of the fact that God is surely beyond
either male or female designations,
and of the inadequacy of language to come up with
simple, quick, and workable solutions.

Help me, O God, to be aware and sensitive
to the problems, hurts, injustices women still
must face in our world. Permit me to play
whatever part I can in the solving of those problems,
the abolition of injustice, the establishment of equality.
Teach me, as a male, to listen and to learn,
rather than leaping in with solutions of my own,
solutions which may only compound matters.
Above all, reveal yourself to me and to your church
as the One in whom both male and female find their
full humanity, move toward their common destiny
in Christ who will set all your people free.

Amen.

DAY SIXTEEN

Luke 13:31–35

MORNING

Go and tell that fox

It strikes me sometimes, especially
when reading defiant words like these,
that not enough is made of the sheer courage
of our Lord. People preach about his gentleness,
they teach about his grace and his compassion,
his generosity and wisdom, but seldom
do I hear a word about the bravery he showed
on this and many other such occasions.

Jesus' ministry, I must remind myself,
was not lived out amid the sunny,
flower-strewn hills of peaceful Galilee.
More and more, as his message became known,
he confronted enemies wherever he appeared,
enemies with one purpose in mind; and that purpose,
his death. He saw what happened to his cousin,
John the Baptist. He must have heard the threats
from Herod, the murmured plottings of the powerful,
dangerous religious leaders of his time.
He knew the fate that lay in store for those
who in any way threatened the harsh peace
imposed by the Roman conquerors.
Yet he defied them all, refused to grant them
any shred of authority over what he said and did,
and persisted in his mission to the end.

He must have known, people are prone to say,
surely he knew—being the Son of God—
that he would triumph in the end.
But such reasoning forgets that he was fully human,
had set aside divinity when he took on mortal flesh.
The man who sweat great drops of blood
in the agony of Gethsemane was not acting out
some divinely prearranged drama in which success
was guaranteed. Furthermore, even if his faith
assured him final victory, the way toward that victory,
the shambling, bloodstained way of the cross,
was an ordeal to be dreaded by any living soul.

Renew in me, Lord God, the realization
and appreciation of the heroism of your Son,
my Savior. Remind me of the need, in these times too,
for courage, that old-fashioned yet demanding virtue.
And strengthen me to face with boldness and true faith
whatever challenges this day may bring.

Amen.

Luke 13:31–35

EVENING

And you would not

There is a strange yet persistent perversity—
maybe this is as close to original sin as we come—
that leads God's children to reject,
thrust away the very healing love
that yet might save them from disaster.

I see it in myself, can recognize such moods
at times when I, in anger or frustration, refuse
to seek, or even to accept when clearly offered to me,
forgiveness, affection, a genuine no-strings-attached
approach to reconciliation with another human being—
my children or my spouse, a colleague
or a neighbor, even a seeming enemy.

What is it in me that prefers
to continue to exist in old hostilities,
to perpetuate situations of alienation and mistrust,
rather than reach out and grasp a hand
held out in generosity and peace?

The Gospels tell that Jesus wept over Jerusalem
and her rejection of God's full and free salvation.
I fear he must weep still over all the foolish ways
I turn aside the daily, almost hourly opportunities
to forget the past, start out afresh, and live
my life in purity and trust.

Can it be the sins I cherish,
love so much that I am reluctant to give up?
I remember reading this brief and yet revealing
prayer of Saint Augustine:

   Lord, make me chaste: but not yet.

Maybe it is pride lodged deep within
which will not permit me to climb down from
my lofty self-esteem enough to admit I need help,
to confess I cannot make it on my own,
to realize my life is in a shambles,
going nowhere, achieving nothing but frustration,
hurt, and injury to others.

Lord, preserve me from myself,
and from my self-defensive, self-destructive
refusals to acknowledge love. Storm my weak defenses,
and gather me to yourself in grace.
Amen.

DAY SEVENTEEN

Genesis 22:1–14

God tested Abraham

This tale has always held a dreadful fascination.
Scholars, poets, philosophers, even psychoanalysts
have long debated the significance of what took place.
Some have suggested Abraham was deluded from the start,
that he tried to emulate the sacrificial practice
of surrounding pagan cults and was finally dissuaded,
but only in the nick of time.

Such explanations—rationalizations?—
are just too easy and convenient.
They dissolve the tension, the horror of the narrative
in a way that robs it of its meaning, even its dignity.
They turn this story into one about a foolish,
perhaps senile, and bloodthirsty old man.
It is surely a mistake, for example, to view this incident
solely through the lens of twentieth-century psychology:
to speculate about the impact on the boy, Isaac,
and his relationship to his father, Abraham.

It is even more misguided to use this tale,
as some have done, in counseling grieving parents
of young children; as if God had called on them
to make a sacrifice similar to Abraham's.
I cannot believe the death of any child
is in accordance with God's will.

Yet this is one of the hardest incidents
in the entire Bible to comprehend.
Are God's servants really tested in such terrible,
harrowing ways? If so, then I certainly would fail.
My faith could never lead me to plunge a knife
into the heart of my own child.

The truth of the matter is, of course,
that that knife was never actually plunged.
Its fatal thrust was halted just before
the downward stroke and the lad was saved,
the test passed, and Abraham's trust was vindicated.
This is, in fact, a story of divine mercy.
Its message: Unlike the pagan deities, Israel's God
does not demand the sacrifice of innocent children.

Help me to understand these scriptures, Lord;
preserve me from clumsy, thoughtless, cruel, foolish,
and even dangerous misinterpretation.

Amen.

Genesis 22:1–14

EVENING

The LORD will provide

I believe we read this story
in the Lenten cycle, not only
for its power and its drama but also
to remind us that God did provide:
that in due time a spotless lamb—
not Abraham's only son, but the Lord's—
was provided to be sacrificed
and show the way to faith and life.

The cross itself has been given many meanings.
Down through the centuries preachers, teachers, poets,
and theologians have sought to mine the richness,

to bring forth from the depths the treasures
hidden in its inexhaustible profundity.

It has been called a demonstration
of the distance that divine love will go
in order to commend itself to our rebellious spirits.
Christ's death has been described as a ransom
paid to Satan so that all God's children might go free.
Others have seen the crucifixion as the payment
of the penalty, incurred by all the sins of humankind;
a penalty which no one else could even attempt
to pay because their own sin canceled out
any benefit that might occur.

Whatever else it was, it was a sacrifice.
That much is clear from words of Jesus in the Gospels.

My body broken for you . . .
My blood poured out for your sake. . . .

Such statements tell me clearly that it was for us
he hung and suffered there, that Jesus' death on Calvary
was for my sake, took place on my behalf.

In these Lenten days, Lord God,
teach me to treasure this new life
he purchased for me with his own. Help me
to live each day in consciousness of the price
that was paid, the cost that was incurred,
the suffering it took to set me free,
to make it possible for me to come to you
in prayer this evening hour.
As much as it is possible, may I be worthy
of the sacrifice; let me live in gratitude that
you did indeed provide, you do provide, the lamb
that saves us now and to the end of time.

Amen.

DAY EIGHTEEN

John 3:1–17

MORNING

You must be born anew

Born again; what a catchphrase
these two words have become for the church,
and what a bone of contention also!
For while Jesus is quite clear on the necessity
of this experience "of water and the Spirit,"
the actual meaning of the expression,
the specific content of this rebirth,
is not quite so obvious.

There are Christians who claim
to know precisely what Jesus meant here,
who would seem to own the patent on rebirth.
They will even break it down into distinct steps
one must take to undergo what they call "second birth."
For such believers being born anew tends to be
a dramatic, emotional, once-in-a-lifetime event,
an intense moment of commitment and conversion
in which one repents one's former life of sin,
invites Jesus into one's heart, and turns one's life
over to his keeping and his lordship.

This is for many a life-transforming experience.
However, there are at least as many others who never know
such a one-time, intense moment of conversion,
yet whose life and work seem just as Christian,
just as faithful as the rest.

Is it right to deny that they too are born again?
For them rebirth is more a lifelong process,
a series of commitments by which
they are continually being led into new life.
It is as if the Spirit brings them into situations,
challenges which are ever new, ever widening,
calling for fresh insight, unanticipated responses,
creative and imaginative actions, somewhat akin
to the experience of birth itself.

There is a sense, Lord, in which,
as I enter this unique new day, I am called
to be reborn in it, to surrender the old securities,
to relinquish the warm, cozy womb of the past,
and to go forth armed only with faith,
my trust in your providence,
my joy in your amazing grace.
Bring me to birth, Lord God, in this
and every day until I put on immortality.

Amen.

John 3:1–17

EVENING

God so loved the world

These words are so familiar,
they conjure chords, rich harmonies
in the inner ear, but people still fail
to grasp their deepest, fullest meaning.
We sing, pray, and preach about how much God
loved the world, and yet we focus that love chiefly
on ourselves. There is comfort in these words,
to be sure, but this is never a comfort to be
clasped exclusively to one's self.

Jesus did not say, "God so loved the church."
Indeed, there was no church as of that date,
only a motley band of followers, common folk

for the most part, and all of them Jews.
Nor did Jesus claim that God loved only Jews,
or the "good people," or even people in general.

It was "the world" that Jesus said God loved
and that he came to save. This is a vital message
which is all too often neglected or ignored.
We focus our concern upon the church,
its preservation, perpetuation, and expansion.
This is our chief priority, and then,
with whatever energy or funds we have left over,
we finally turn to look out there at the world,
its needs, its problems, and its crises.

They write of the earliest Christians
that they "turned the world upside down."
Will they write of Christians in my time that
they turned the church upside down, or inside out,
so that, instead of being here to serve and save
God's world, we believe the Christian's goal
is to love and serve the church; and the world may
go to hell, as it seems bent on doing?

Restore to me tonight, Lord God,
bright joy in your creation, the delight
within my bones at all the loveliness and grandeur
of the cosmos. Fill me with new compassion
for all who suffer, with indignation at injustice,
with determination to do whatever I can
to halt the mad destruction of our environment.
Teach me to love your world as you do, Lord,
and to care for it in your name.

Amen.

DAY NINETEEN

Psalm 95

MORNING

O come, let us sing to the LORD

These psalms are full of the sound of music.
Everywhere I turn in this great book I find people
making what the psalmist calls "a joyful noise."
At times even the rest of creation—mountains and hills,
forests and oceans, stars in their courses, the heavens
themselves—join in one great hymn of praise.

Music is such a blessed and mysterious gift.
It speaks to me, for me, on a level beyond words alone.
It can express the depths of sorrow, the heat of rage
and fury, the tenderness of true affection,
the tranquil peace of quiet meditation.
And when I lift my voice in praise,
unite with fellow worshipers and the mighty organ
in a rousing hymn of glad thanksgiving,
I am lifted far beyond myself, my own narrow concerns,
and take my place with all the hosts of heaven
and earth around God's high and holy throne
singing "Glory . . . glory . . . glory!"

As I meditate this Sunday morning,
I anticipate the music I will soon be sharing
as I enter the Lord's house to worship
in the company of faith. I am thankful for
the many gifts through which this blessing reaches me:
for organists and choir directors, singers

and musicians, handbell ringers and also those
who give their time and talent to teach
little children how to know and share these joys.

Most of all I thank my God
for the music in my soul, those basic
inner harmonies of grace and joy and laughter
beyond tears which underlie the surface clamor,
all the mad and frantic din and call me,
by the lilting of a melody, a catch or two
of verse, a sudden unexpected birdsong,
into God's presence, into rest
within God's peace.

As I worship you this holy day, Lord God,
speak to me, sing to me in the music
I will hear. Then tune my heart, my life,
to resonate a pure and glorious tone
of living praise.
              Amen.

Psalm 95

EVENING

Harden not your hearts

Worship with a soft heart
is no easy matter; there are so many factors,
influences which tend toward a stubborn
and unyielding attitude of hardness.

There are distractions which draw my thoughts
away from listening for God's inner voice:
petty little complaints about surroundings,
the temperature, the flower arrangements,
the choice of hymns, behavior of my neighbors,
or their children in the pews.
On the other hand I can get so caught up
in the beauty of the music, the glowing splendor

of stained glass, the literary elegance of prayers,
scripture readings, even the eloquent delivery
of the preacher, that I never hear the living word,
never even notice the hand knocking at
the tight-shut door of my soul.

Beyond distractions are defenses,
deliberate and devious ways in which I seek
to prevent myself from getting too involved,
from being reached and moved to action
by the message that I hear. Over the years
I have perfected these techniques until
they are almost automatic, subliminal.
I hear about the suffering of the hungry
and remind myself I sent a check last Christmas.
Corruption and injustice, the problems
of pollution, are all countered by
"What can one person do?"
As for the call to personal morality,
to responsibility and honesty and faithfulness,
I tend to wallow in my guilt rather than seeking
ways for the divine transforming grace to work
its miracles upon my life.

In the silence of this evening hour,
restore my listening ear.
Remind me of the joy of my salvation,
the shining hope and vision in which I once began
this pilgrimage of faith. Then speak to me
your tender word that comforts and renews.
Soften my heart, O Lord, that it might yield
again to your bright, saving grace.
Amen.

DAY TWENTY

John 4:5–42

MORNING

Sir, give me this water

This is a fascinating dialogue.
The woman is so direct and down-to-earth,
at least at the beginning of the conversation.

> How is it that you, a Jew, ask a drink of me, a woman of Samaria?
> ... Sir, you have nothing to draw with, and the well is deep; where do
> you get that living water? ... Sir, give me this water, that I may not thirst,
> nor come here to draw.

It is as if she insists on keeping things
on the level of the practical, while Jesus seeks
to pierce beyond to something far deeper.
Then, when Jesus moves to the everyday
by asking her about her husband,
she is the one who wants to talk theology,
to discuss the proper place to worship.
It is somewhat like a chess match,
or fencing, with its rapier thrusts and parries.

I find myself liking this woman,
for all her sorry past, and there is
an underlying feeling in this narrative
that leads me to suspect that Jesus liked her too,
found her skillful resistance a worthy challenge
to his powers of persuasion.
She reminds me of that other woman,
the one from Syro-Phoenicia, whose clever

rejoinder about the dogs eating the crumbs
beneath the master's table brought healing
and new hope to her sick daughter.

So often we Christians feel
that the only appropriate response to God
is one of abject guilt, humility, or pious prattle.
These quick-witted women, and Abraham too,
who argued with the Lord over the fate of Sodom,
suggest that the Creator might actually like us
to be more ourselves. God made us as we are,
gave us minds to reason with, tongues to join debate.
Is it right that we should always wear
a false face in the divine presence?

Teach me the difference, Lord, between
true honesty and blasphemy, that I may address
you as my Father, yet respect you as my God.

Amen.

John 4:5–42

EVENING

Come, see a man who told me all that I ever did

She did not hesitate an instant
to share the good news with her neighbors,
but left her water jar at the well
and went back to bring the people out to Jesus.
She was just as direct with them as she had been
with him, and her directness led them
to "the Savior of the world."

What is it about my faith
makes it so difficult for me
to follow the example of that woman?
Why is it that I can speak freely about sports
or local politics, the latest entertainment
or the state of the world, and yet become

completely tongue-tied when it comes to talk
about salvation and my faith in Jesus Christ?

Perhaps it is that such talk is so personal,
involves such intimate matters of heart and soul,
that I am reluctant to include such words
in casual conversation. Certainly to barge right in
on total strangers with such topics seems to me
to risk doing more harm to the gospel
than it could possibly do good.

Yet there are appropriate times and places,
proper settings where it is only natural
to tell about the wellsprings of my faith,
about the hope and trust that motivate
the very best that is within me.
And all too often on such occasions also
I find myself without the courage
of my own convictions, unable to say a word
about the faith that I hold dear.

Forgive me, Lord,
that I should ever be ashamed
of you and of your word of life.
Teach me how to speak a word, a quiet,
honest, genuine word—not shrill or in any way
self-righteous or condemning, but with conviction
and concern—a word of love that seeks simply
to share the best that I have found in life
with those I cherish as my friends.
Lord, show me how to share the love you give to me.

Amen.

DAY TWENTY-ONE

Exodus 20:1–17

MORNING

No other gods before me

That seems to be what all these
ten commandments boil down to in the end:
God's total claim on my allegiance.
"I am the LORD your God," they state—
right at the outset—and all that follows
is a working out of the implications
of that introductory statement.

The first five laws direct themselves
to my relationship to God, defining what
I must and must not do in order to maintain
the covenant between us. Each one seems simple
in and of itself: keeping the Sabbath, not taking
the divine name in vain, and so forth. Yet each law
holds a claim which goes much further
than first reading might suggest.

For example, I could read the forbidding
of any other gods to mean I must not worship sun
or moon or any of the pagan pantheon of deities.
And, to be sure, that is at least a part of
what this great commandment signifies.
But "other gods" can mean much more
than following false religions.
There are idols that I worship,
around which I build my life, my dreams,

my values, far more dangerous to me
than any cultic figures from the past.

There is the god Success,
which laid its eager claims upon me
from my early years, demands the sacrifice
of time and energy and talent. Even family
must yield before its stern priorities,
along with any high ideals of honesty,
integrity, fidelity, and fair play.

The gods of Comfort, of Acceptance,
and Acclaim require their offerings too,
as do Sexual Adventure and the ever popular Fun.
Even the lofty god called Holiness can be
a crafty rival to the Lord's exclusive claim.

Re-form my life this day around this ancient pattern
you have set, my Lord, and save me from false gods.

Amen.

Exodus 20:1–17

EVENING

You shall not covet

The second five commandments follow from the first,
but here the focus shifts from relationship to God
to my relationships with fellow human beings.

Of all of these the one I have most trouble with
is this: "Thou shalt not covet. . . ."
Bearing false witness can also be a problem,
not so much in law courts as in the cruel
daily tribunals of idle conversation.
Honoring parents becomes exceedingly complicated
in today's mobile and rootless society.
Even stealing and killing may become areas of concern

as one looks at one's participation in government,
foreign policy, national defense, society as a whole.

But coveting is where I trip and fall most easily.
In fact, the world about me—in TV commercials,
newspapers, and the glossy magazines, in films, plays,
novels too—seems like one massive invitation,
provocation to this act of coveting.
"Wouldn't you like to own one of these," they ask,
"to drive, taste, live in, wear, enjoy—all of these?"
That is the message beamed, or even blasted out,
in my direction every day, in countless ways.
And it all encourages me to covet
something I do not already own;
it all works to create in me dissatisfaction
with what I have right now.

Oh, it may not literally be my *neighbor's* house
or car, new boat, or sexual partner, as stated
in the tablets of the law, that I lust after.
But this commandment judges me for my participation
in the frantic buying and spending,
the unrelenting consumerism of these times.

Deliver me, Lord, from the endless desire to acquire,
the urge to heap possessions on possessions.
Set me free to enjoy the blessings
I already have received: this world in all its wonder,
my friends and family, my church, this self
you have entrusted to me with all its possibilities
and challenges. And fix my eyes on you,
and on the prize you have prepared:
life eternal in your presence and your grace.

Amen.

DAY TWENTY-TWO

1 Corinthians 1:22–25

MORNING

For Jews demand signs

I'm not sure why Paul picked out the Jews.
Certainly, today, all sorts of people look for signs
and proofs, demand demonstrations, even miracles
to convince them that the word is true and valid.

In our modern scientific world,
where facts must be established in the laboratory
and by the experimental method, people respond
with weary skepticism to the gospel's call
for faith and trust. "Only believe . . ."
smacks too much of the used car lot,
those scams in the mail and on TV.
This is a hard-bitten generation; they seek
iron-clad guarantees before making commitments.

And yet God offers a vast range of signs:
in the never-ending splendors of creation;
the selfless tenderness of human love;
the persistent, sacrificial service of the saints
and of the church across the centuries; above all,
in that One who raised his cross on Calvary's hill,
a sign of death turned into life—
God gives us signs.

The trouble is we pick and choose the signs we heed.
Someone has written that if God should rearrange the stars

one night so that they spelled out "God Loves You"
across the sky in vivid color, folk would be impressed,
might even change their ways awhile—a week, a month,
even a year—but eventually the words would grow familiar,
we would get used to seeing them up there,
they would become to us just another constellation,
and we would revert to the ways we lived before.

This morning as I rose I was greeted by signs
of your providential care, Lord: sunlight and birdsong,
family and friendship, nourishment for the body,
news for the mind, a brief snatch of solitude
to refresh the soul. Direct my eyes to these,
to all that they are telling me about this new day
I begin right now, Lord God.
Then lead me past all signs to the reality
of your presence, your plan and purpose for me
in these hours ahead. And teach me
how to truly say
                    Amen.

1 Corinthians 1:22–25

EVENING

The foolishness of God

What a daring expression this is of Paul's!
To call God a fool is beyond the courage
of most Christians in any generation,
but then Paul certainly went beyond most Christians
in his insight and perception of the gospel.

Earlier Paul writes about the folly of "the cross"
and of "Christ crucified" and, to tell the truth,
from an objective viewpoint it does seem utter madness
to seek to save the world by being executed as a criminal.
Jesus' repeated message about finding life through
losing it, receiving life by giving it away,
sounds positively suicidal when taken out of context.

While the entire message of his Sermon on the Mount,
with its celebration of the meek, the poor,
the persecuted, can only be a recipe for failure
in the kind of world I live in.

I suppose that's where the difference lies.
For Jesus was not talking about, was not seeking
to describe, the kind of world I live in.
What he had in mind, what he set out to build,
was the kind of world that God might want to live in—
a world that is everywhere a temple for the divine,
a world that will express God's plan for us,
that destiny for which God conceived
and carried out creation in the first place.

From the point of view of this world—
with its falseness, its failures upon failures
compounded over many generations, its violence and fear,
callousness and greed—the way of the cross,
of self-sacrificial love, is foolishness indeed.

But in the light of eternity,
in the radiance that shines from this old book
and from the lives, that one true Life that is
set forth here, I can perceive another world:
an alternative to all the sad betrayals,
shoddy compromises of the past; a fairer, truer,
realm where love fulfills itself in selflessness
and joy is born wherever life is shared.

Teach me such foolishness, Lord God,
and fit me for your world which is to be.

Amen.

DAY TWENTY-THREE

Exodus 3:1–5

MORNING

I will turn aside

Some have argued that the miracle here
lies not so much in the bush which burned,
yet was not burned up, as in the fact
that Moses turned aside to see it.
Elizabeth Barrett Browning wrote:

> Earth's crammed with heaven,
> and every common bush afire with God;
> But only he who sees takes off his shoes,
> The rest sit round it and pluck blackberries.

Certainly this world is filled with marvels enough
to cause even the busiest to halt and pay attention.
Yet we become hardened to beauty,
just as we do to ugliness.
Our minds are preoccupied, taken up in advance
by the deadly serious business of daily bread.
So that when God calls from an early blossoming magnolia,
in a child's invitation to a game,
a moment of spring sunlight, or even in the distant
chime of church bells Sunday morning, we shut it out,
avert our eyes, deny the beckoning of life,
love, and mystery, and set grim shoulders
squarely to the grinding wheel again.

What if Moses had been like me, I wonder.
What if he had said, "I'd like to stop, check out

that strangely burning bush, but the sheep are moving on;
I cannot leave them unattended. Maybe I'll have
a chance to catch it on the journey home."

Was it curiosity alone that made Moses turn aside?
Or had his sudden flight, his concern over
the suffering of his captive people,
his long exile in the wilderness,
taught him an awareness of the divine presence,
an openness to God's voice, that seems impossible
in the crush and hustle of my harried days?

Open my eyes and ears this morning, Lord.
Attune all my senses, that I might recognize your call
when it comes to me today; in the need of a stranger,
or the companionship of a friend,
the words of an old song, an item in the news,
an open door to silence, a bush that burns
yet never is burned up. Then let me turn aside
and give heed to what you have to say.

Amen.

Exodus 3:1–5

EVENING

Put off your shoes from your feet

Some years ago I visited Al Aksa,
the mosque of Omar, beneath that glorious
golden Dome of the Rock, high above Jerusalem.
As we approached the ancient shrine
I noticed, scattered by the doors, heaps of shoes
from the feet of all who entered; and we too,
in turn, had to walk around that shrine in only socks.
I can still recall the off-balance,
vaguely uneasy feeling this produced,
and I suspect this old custom is intended
to have precisely that effect; to see that

no one feels too sure of him- or herself
in the presence of divinity.

I see two quite divergent strands
in the teachings of the faith about the Lord,
two quite opposite emphases which, for all their
contradiction, correspond to two persuasions
drawn from my own experience.
On the one hand I am told God is majestic, dreadful,
the Almighty, in whose presence all human flesh
must tremble; on the other I learn God is most intimate
and tender, One who loves me as a parent loves,
leads me as a shepherd leads the flock.

To select one or the other view would be
to lessen the reality of what and who God is.
Even Jesus in his parables describes the Lord
both as loving Father and as mighty King,
as humble housewife and as Lord of the vineyard.
So too in Exodus, this familiar
yet mysterious narrative of the call of Moses,
God appears at first as the mighty, ancient Lord
of Moses' ancestors, and Moses hides his face in fear.
But then this holy, awesome One speaks of compassion,
of heartache for the sufferings of his people,
and Moses is led from fear to dedication
as he is sent forth in service
to set his people free.

Preserve me, Lord God, in these my prayers,
from any easy, breezy, overfamiliar approach to you.
Humble me before your divine majesty; but permit me
still to know your firm hand upon my shoulder,
your strong love about my heart.

Amen.

DAY TWENTY-FOUR

John 2:13–22

MORNING

Making a whip of cords, he drove them all

People wield this passage as a weapon
in seeking to refute Christian pacifists,
all those who preach a gospel of nonviolence.
They cite these words as evidence that Jesus, himself,
employed violence and therefore "Turn the other cheek"
is not to be applied or required in every situation.
If the cause be righteous, such persons would argue,
then a certain amount of violence may be justified.

It seems to me there is a danger
in trying to derive general ethical principles,
especially related to such a vital issue as this one,
on the basis of isolated incidents in the Gospels,
of individual events in Jesus' life.
The portrayal of our Lord in the New Testament,
confusing though it be in places, can hardly
be described as that of a person open to violence.
Compassion is the dominating quality
that I perceive, a compassion so strong,
so nonviolent, that he can even pray for those
who hammer nails through his hands and feet.
Yet there was anger in him;
he could not have been human without
that possibility, and every now and then
it briefly flashes forth in righteous indignation.

Was this a failure on his part?
Could Jesus have known sin when he felt anger?

I read about your anger, O God—
your wrath, as it is called—in many places
in the Bible. And just as your love
is somewhat like but far beyond any experience
of love that I can know, so must your holy anger
be quite different from these sullen moods
and tantrums I experience.

The enigmas of divine wrath and mercy,
the balancing of your justice with your grace,
is beyond the penetration of my mind. I only know
that the holy, righteous wrath which blazed forth
in the temple was never uncontrolled, like mine,
was ever in the service of your mercy
and your truth: that mercy and that truth
in which I now begin this day.

Amen.

John 2:13–22

EVENING

You shall not make my father's house a house of trade

The holiness of Almighty God is a quality
hard for me to experience, let alone comprehend.
From childhood I have been taught to regard the Lord
as a friend, a helper, shepherd, one who cares
for me like a father, who loves me
as a mother does her child.

Yet in the scriptures, in the life of Jesus,
I catch glimpses of another side, another aspect
of the divine being which by its very nature
must judge and then condemn the shabby, sinful ways
I walk in. The Psalms, the book of Job, present God
as One whose purity and majesty tower so far

above my human frame that I can only kneel
in trembling awe before the Presence—
more than awe, in fear.

There is a purity in God which,
without the shielding of the cross of grace,
would destroy with one clean glance my compromised
and fatally flawed nature. I believe it was
that quality of pure holiness which burst forth
in Jesus when he saw those dealers in the temple,
so that he could not tolerate the sight another instant
but swept them forth like dust before a broom.

As I kneel before your searching presence
this night, Almighty One, I begin to recognize
the temple trafficking that I am guilty of,
the trashing of the holy things, the price
that I have put, at least allowed to be placed,
upon my loyalty, my integrity, my self.
I see the ways I may have used my claims
to faith, at times, to win unfair advantage;
the deals, the many and convenient deals I have made
that traded purity or principle for power
or pleasure, momentary gain.

Drive out the money changers, the compromisers,
merchandisers from their slick control over my days.
Confront me with the clean, clear vision
of your high demand for my perfection.
Show me again the heights to which,
in Christ, you bid me climb;
and touch me with your purifying fire.

Amen.

DAY TWENTY-FIVE

Psalm 19:7–14

The law of the LORD is perfect

The writer of this psalm
has been thinking of the sun and the life
it brings to all it touches; and that thought
leads him to the law and to the way
that it "refreshes the soul."

Today the law is seldom seen as a source
of life and light. Laws of the state tend to be viewed
as a necessary nuisance, encroaching on liberty,
yet needed to hold back the tides of anarchy and chaos.
The laws of God too are regarded, all too often,
in similar fashion. Even many of those
who call themselves believers see the Ten Commandments,
the ethical instructions of the Bible, as a burden
to be borne, an imposition to be struggled with
in order to achieve God's grace and favor.

To the Hebrew people the law was a great gift.
They sensed their privilege in being entrusted with
such teachings, being elected to live out before
all nations the true and proper way of life.
Rather than crushing or defeating the human spirit,
they saw the law reviving it: lifting it from
the chaos and confusion of a life devoid of values,
purpose, meaning and setting it on the true way,
the path of life and genuine prosperity.

Just as the sun in the physical world
brings light and health, direction to all life,
so in the world of the spirit God's law blesses
all it touches—"rejoicing the heart,"
as the psalmist sings. It is as if,
exploring the attic, one found a game
complete with all the parts except the rules.
Without those rules, however, nothing is possible
beyond the pointless shuffling of pieces.

Deliver me, Lord, from such emptiness.
Show me—though saved by grace—how I still need
to live the Christian life according to your teachings
or it is no life at all. Help me to claim
the hidden treasures of your law as the shaper
and the guide of all I do, all I become.
Thus may I walk—by faith—
in the paths you have marked out for me.

Amen.

Psalm 19:7–14

EVENING

Acceptable in thy sight

This little prayer tucked in
at the close of a majestic psalm
seems to breathe with the pure, true spirit
of the psalmist of ancient Israel.

Having crafted a poem of immortal beauty,
a meditation whose profundity will never be surpassed,
this author's only wish is not for fame
or literary reputation,
not for lofty philosophical recognition
or acclaim, but for acceptance "in thy sight":
that his work may find a place
within God's purposes.
Such a sentiment strikes me

as the purest form of modesty;
yet far more than modesty is at work here.
This writer has actually learned—
discovered to be true in his own life—
the secret that he writes about.
He realizes that this whole creation—
the starry heavens, the radiant sun,
the teachings and the wisdom
of his temple worship and his faith—
all these exist for one sole splendid purpose:
to show forth the praise and glory of God.

In light of this discovery, the only hope,
the highest dream he can conceive,
is that his work—his words and meditations—
might take their proper place,
play their own part, however small,
in the great, thankful song of majesty and joy
that is the hymn of all creation.

My prayers this night too,
however slow and faltering, reluctant
to begin, resistant to serious concentration,
these stumbling words and meditations of my own
must somehow have a part to play, a note to sound,
perhaps even a chord to be completed
in that eternal anthem.

Even so, Lord, let the words of my mouth
and these meditations of my heart be acceptable
in thy sight, O my rock and my redeemer.
                                        Amen.

DAY TWENTY-SIX

2 Corinthians 5:16–21

MORNING

The old has passed away, behold, the new has come

A new creation in Christ.
I have a difficult time seeing myself,
conceiving of my own struggle between faith and doubt,
in such clear-cut and absolute terms as these.
This text describes the Christian
as one in whom "the old has passed away,"
and I wish that could be true of me and yet
there is still so much of oldness in my ways.

I look back across the years
this Sunday morning, and I can detect
so little change, so few measurable improvements
over the old, recalcitrant me who offered
his life to Christ so many years ago.
The bright promises I made, to God and to myself,
seem to have fallen by the wayside;
the clear vision I once held of purity
and goodness has been obscured by the deposits
of moments and of months as they pass by.
The hope I cherished of a daily closer walk with God
has become submerged in all the busyness
of career and family life.
Yet I struggle on somehow, still seeking
to find a faith that is secure, unshakable,
to know an inner light that will fill my days
with heaven, shine forth God's grace to all I meet.

Looking at this text more carefully,
I realize that it is not meant to guide my attitude
toward myself, my evaluation of the state of my own soul,
with its tendency to always see the worst.
This word about a new creation tells me, rather,
how I am to look upon my fellow Christians.
It suggests, when I regard another person, I should see
not a collection of human fallibilities and flaws,
the sum total of our common mortal weakness,
but rather should see Christ, who gave himself for all,
and stands in healing reconciliation now,
not just between us and our God
but between each one of us and our neighbors.

Deliver me, Lord, from the spiritual arrogance
which makes me judge myself and my fellow believers
more harshly than you have done in Christ.
Help me to see, and then to live your new creation.

Amen.

2 Corinthians 5:16–21

EVENING

So we are ambassadors for Christ

What a title!
To be honest, it makes me alternate
between terror and a sense of enormous privilege.

I notice that Paul doesn't say we ought to be
but that we *are* ambassadors. In other words,
whatever we say or do reflects in credit
or in blame upon the Lord in person.
Because I claim the name of Christ,
however I might seek to qualify and hedge about
that claim within the privacy of my own soul,
the world will see me as a representative,
an example of what the Christian faith
looks like in daily life. And that realization

is enough to bring dismay to the heart
of any reasonably honest person.

On the other hand, to a person like myself,
whose life, at times, seems dull and humdrum,
bound in the shallows and backwaters of existence,
such a statement, such a "job description"—
ambassador for Christ, representative on earth
of the kingdom of heaven—is more than sufficient
to lift one's days from any sense of meaningless routine
and set them down afresh within the boundaries of eternity,
the bright horizons of God's universal destiny.

To be called upon, in all one does, to present
the claims, pursue the policies of the King of kings
and Lord of lords is no easy undertaking.
But what a glorious way to spend one's days,
what a magnificent cause in which to pour out
freely, even prodigally, all one's energies,
talents, imagination, and intellect!
We Christians are in the foreign service,
charged in every instant of our living,
every atom of our being, with the task
of letting Christ shine through:
his peace into a world of warring nations,
his reconciliation wherever families or communities
are divided and set apart. As Paul puts it:

God making his appeal through us.

Grant me the courage and the vision, Lord, to see
and claim this high calling in Christ's name.

Amen.

DAY TWENTY-SEVEN

Psalm 34:1–8

MORNING

My soul makes its boast in the LORD

Boasting tends to be frowned upon nowadays.
Oh, the proud parent or grandparent
can pass around the latest family pictures,
the sports fan can proclaim "We're number one!"
but any more than this is usually unacceptable.
One simply does not call attention
to one's own achievements. Or does one?

While blatant self-advertisement
is certainly looked down on as distasteful,
a host of far more subtle ways exist by which
people nowadays let others know they are important.
There are the kind of clothes you wear or car you drive,
the cool and casual mention of your alma mater,
the furtive yet ingenious ways we find to sprinkle
every conversation with little gems of information,
clues by which any sophisticated listener
will realize he or she is listening
to someone of weight and stature,
someone well worth listening to.

Much of all this, of course,
is quite innocuous: an attempt, perhaps,
to create a good impression, little more.
Problems arise, however, when attempts like these
begin to cross the line between fact and fantasy,

or when the impression one seeks to create
becomes so all-important and consuming
that the real person is swallowed up.

The perfect antidote is found here
in Psalm 34, where the writer,
in a hymn of praise and thanksgiving,
sings forth the boasting of his soul in God.
To boast in God is not to claim unique
or special favors, nor is it to enumerate
at great length the lurid sins from which the Lord
has set you free. To boast in God is rather
to show forth with every ounce of being
the reality and wonder of our Lord,
to permit one's life to become a vessel,
into which and from which the grace of God is poured.

Deliver me from false pretensions, Lord.
Become this day my boast, my pride, my joy.

Amen.

Psalm 34:1–8

EVENING

O taste and see that the LORD is good!

I like that invitation to *taste*
the reality and the goodness of the Lord.

We modern-day Christians tend to confine
the experience of God almost entirely to the mind—
the realm of thinking, conceiving, believing—
rather than the physical world of tasting,
touching, feeling. Someone has written that
if today's believers were portrayed in terms of
the sense organs used in their faith, they would be
represented in the form of an enormous ear.
We hear the word, consider it in our brains,

weigh the pros and cons, and then decide
whether to accept it or not.

The biblical writers were much more sensuous
in their approach to God. They spoke of the Holy One
as a being who could be not only heard
but seen and even touched, tasted, and smelled.
When Jesus, on the evening of Easter Day,
appeared before the eyes of his astonished followers,
he urged them, "Handle me and see."
"Reach out your hand," he said to Thomas,
"and thrust it in my side."
And in that holiest of moments,
when mystery became embodied in a sacred meal,
our Lord said, "Take and eat, this is my body . . .
my blood," and moved this faith of ours
far beyond the limited confines of the mind
into the full, complete reality of life itself
in all its rainbow spectrum of experience.

In these daily times of prayer
and meditation, Lord, show me how to begin
to expand my own experience of you
beyond the mental realm and into the physical.
In my posture as I kneel to pray, stand to praise,
and sit to meditate upon your word; in my awareness
of the creatures and the creations all about me—
the rug, table, books, and plants, the scene
beyond the windowpane; in the food which,
by your grace, I eat; in the touch of the wind,
the fragrance of the seasons, the gestures of love,
reveal your own self in all your splendor.
Teach me to taste and see your goodness, Lord.

Amen.

DAY TWENTY-EIGHT

Luke 15:1–3, 11–24

MORNING

This man receives sinners and eats with them

You can judge a person
by the company he or she keeps.

I'm sure that saying was as widely accepted
back in Jesus' time as it is now.
Therefore it is not at all surprising
that when Jesus insisted on spending time,
healing, eating meals, even lodging at the homes
of the lowest of the low, the sort of people
no one who is anyone would be caught dead with,
he would be accused of being one of them,
an outcast and a sinner.

In actual fact, of course, he was neither.
He knew no sin, despite experiencing all the trials
and temptations every human being faces.
And, far from an outcast, Jesus was the only person
who truly and fully belonged in this world
of God's creating. All the rest of them, and us too—
all the others were the outcasts; and he had come,
the son and rightful heir, to bring the outcasts back,
restore them to the family and household of God.
People judge us by the company we keep.
When the church, whether by design or not,
separates or segregates itself from any class
of people, any category of sinner, then it fails

to be Christ's church and becomes our private club.
This has been a failing from the days of the
New Testament epistles, this tendency to gather
into cliques and factions sharing similar opinions,
tastes, or income levels. It's as if we all need
someone to look down upon, some class or group
we can believe inferior to ourselves.

Yet the church of Jesus of Nazareth—
this man who only seemed at home with the lowest
of the low, with those who could look down
on no one at all—the church exists to tear down
such divisions, to set each and every living soul
on the same level, as both lost sinner and
saint redeemed by God's good grace.

Redeem the company I keep this day, good Lord.
Define it only by the limits of your love.

Amen

Luke 15:1–3, 11–24

EVENING

But while he was yet at a distance

What a picture we glimpse
in these few words! There is the boy,
doggedly tramping the last few, familiar miles,
reciting, repeating over and over to himself
the speech he had prepared so carefully
when he set out upon this shameful, sad return:

> Father, I have sinned against heaven and before you; I am no longer
> worthy to be called your son; treat me as one of your hired servants.

And there is the father, waiting and watching,
as he has done so many mornings in the past, straining
his now fading eyes to see far down the dusty road
and catch the first sign of that homecoming

he has prayed for ever since his younger son
took off for parts unknown.

And now a speck comes into view,
and then a shape, a figure, a walk, a pace
that is still achingly familiar, a stride that tugs
the cords of memory far back to the very first
tottering steps that boy had ever taken,
steps into his father's outstretched arms.
He runs to greet him, stumbles—shaking between
hope and fear of what he might confront—hastens down
that road until his son is in his arms again:
no time for explanations or regrets, no room within
that vast embrace for prepared speeches,
carefully considered proposals,
only the tears of joy reborn, the words,
warm from the heart, of happy welcome.
"Quick, the best robe . . . a ring . . . and shoes . . .
and kill the fatted calf . . . for this my son
was dead and is alive again; he was lost,
and is found."
So many parents, children too,
have lived or prayed to live this scene
in their own lives and broken relationships.
The kingdom, Jesus tells us here, is all about
reunion, reconciliation, and homecoming;
is all wrapped up in love which makes
even forgiveness only secondary;
is all caught up in tears of joy which lead
inevitably to a great celebration.

Help me, Lord, to share the joy of both
this father and this son, to find myself swept up
into the arms of your bright overwhelming grace.

Amen.

DAY TWENTY-NINE

1 Samuel 16:1–13

MORNING

How long will you grieve over Saul?

These stories from the early days of Israel,
when the idea of kingship was the subject for long
and fierce debate, make fascinating reading.

It is possible to study them and perceive
two quite opposing points of view.
The first suggests that the institution
of the monarchy was a popular demand of the people,
that they might be like the other nations round about;
and Samuel, acting in God's name, anointed Saul—
a mistaken move from the beginning—
with extreme reluctance and dire foreboding.

But another strand is seen in these old tales
that whispers of a divine choice that went wrong,
that presents Saul in towering, heroic terms at first,
but then detects a tragic flaw which brings him down
despite himself. There is something Shakespearean
about the character of Saul, a flavor of Othello
or Macbeth about the driven, almost fated way
he brings about his own destruction;
about the relationship of protégé-turned-rival,
the insane jealousy yet underlying respect,
even affection that persists between
this first king and his gallant captain, David.

When the Lord, in this text, asks Samuel
how long he will grieve over Saul, we catch
yet another glimpse of the attraction of the man
and the lingering sadness of his downfall.
There is, in Israel's memory, an underlying sympathy
for this torn, distracted human being, who sets out
so full of promise and ends up in dark despair,
violent insanity, and bitter death.

Tales like these in holy scripture
convey no simplistic, tag-line lessons
with the moral of the story spelled out in big red letters.
They deal, instead, with the whole mystery of human life
and divine destiny. They lead us through the heights
and deepest depths of human fear and courage,
loyalty and betrayal, faith and folly.
They illustrate trust in God in the midst
of a confused, complex world. Grant to me, Lord,
the wisdom and the grace of such a trust.

Amen.

1 Samuel 16:1–13

EVENING

The LORD sees not as man sees

I can imagine old Samuel
getting more and more exasperated.
His entire mission was impossibly dangerous—
to anoint a new king while the old one was still
set firmly, and even violently, on the throne.

The alibi he had been given might well
get him inside the gates of Bethlehem,
but it certainly would not explain the horn of oil
he carried for anointing, nor the little ceremony
God seemed to have in mind for one of Jesse's sons.

And now it seemed, despite outward appearances,
that none of the sons would do after all.
He could have sworn that Eliab was the one;
his lofty stature and handsome, rugged frame
might put even Saul himself in the shade.
And then Abinadab and Shammah,
all seven of the men in Jesse's house,
and each one of them passed over by the Lord.
What could El Shaddai, Lord of hosts,
be thinking of? Surely this was not to be
another fiasco like the one with Saul.

Then the youngest boy is brought,
called in from the hillside where he tends
the family flocks, and even as he walks in the door
old Samuel's heart leaps up in joy.
This one, this David, is the lad that God has chosen,
no possible doubt about it, and Samuel spills out
the sacred oil upon his head in a moment
of shocked and holy astonishment.

The rest of the story, of Goliath and of Jonathan,
Abner and Absalom, Bathsheba, Uriah, and Nathan,
is an epic that still enchants the mind,
heart, and soul of every reader.
Yet it all begins in this unlikely moment
as a young lad comes in from work and finds himself
at the heart of God's great plan for humankind.

Lord, whatever destiny you have in store for me
help me to greet it with the simple trust
of the boy who wrote so long ago:

> The Lord is my shepherd,
> I shall not want.

                    Amen.

DAY THIRTY

John 9

MORNING

He saw a man blind from his birth

"Father, Mother, I can see!"
the first words I ever spoke in church,
when, at nine or ten years old, I played the part
of this blind man in a Sunday school production.
It was a long time ago now,
in a little Congregational chapel
in the North of England,
but I have never forgotten those words
and the excitement I experienced in saying them.

Looking back, I wonder why
this all seemed so important to me.
Was it just the thrill of being on the stage?
Or was there something more,
something about that story, the healing
that took place in it, the One who did the healing,
that touched me in an unforgettable way?

I read the tale again this morning
and am struck by its natural and realistic tone.
The dialogue does not sound artificial
or in any way contrived,
but just the matter-of-fact kind of things
I can imagine people would say in such a situation.
I appreciate the young man's honesty
before his questioners, the Pharisees,

and his eventual impatience with their badgering
that leads him to retort:
"Whether or not he is a sinner, it is not
my business to tell. One thing I do know,
however; I was blind and now I can see."
He sticks to the plain and obvious facts
of the case as he knows them, and in so doing
is led to the feet of the Master.

Too often in my life the plain facts
get submerged below the trimmings and the verbiage.
I am confronted with human need, like Jesus
in this incident, and immediately find a dozen
or more reasons why I am not able to respond
in an immediate and directly helpful way.
Remove, O Lord, these thick protective lenses
that shield me from your presence and your call;
grant me a clean, uncluttered view of all
that happens in this day, that I might
recognize and serve your kingdom.
                                        Amen.

John 9

EVENING

You do not know where he comes from

Throughout this fascinating narrative
the writer of this Gospel is contrasting
two kinds of darkness and
two kinds of light.

First we meet the physical darkness,
the blindness which has afflicted this young man
from his birth, and which, as Jesus tells
his disciples, is not a punishment for sin
but an opportunity for God's grace.
This kind of darkness is readily dispelled
by the power of the incarnate Word

and the obedience of the blind man.
He sees the light of day
and is also led to recognize
the light of the world:

Lord, I believe.

The other darkness in this tale
is not so easily dispelled.
The blindness of those who see,
yet do not see, will not even accept
the healing cure when it is offered.
The irony within these dialogues
is skillfully brought out as the healed one
says, in effect, to his accusers,
"I was blind, but now I can see.
You can see and yet remain completely blind."

In terms of the question
at the beginning of this incident,
Jesus seems to be saying that
the blindness which is the result of sin
is not a physical but a spiritual affliction.
It is a curse one brings upon oneself,
a darkness of the soul one must choose to undergo
by refusing to accept that light
which is the gift of God.

As the darkness of this evening hour
gathers around me, Lord, let your light,
the radiance of your holy word, that inner light
which is your truth, the fiery flame of the Spirit,
and the eternal glory of the Christ illumine
the deep shadows and guide me till I rest in peace.

Amen.

DAY THIRTY-ONE

2 Chronicles 36:14–23

MORNING

Therefore he brought up against them

A whole understanding of history,
a whole attempt to comprehend calamity
and disaster, is contained in these few verses
at the close of the book of Chronicles.

The people of Judah and Jerusalem
have experienced crushing defeat at the hands
of the Babylonians. Their capital city
has been leveled, their temple has been sacked,
and their fellow citizens have either been
mercilessly slaughtered or led off
into captivity in a strange land.

In a time when theology reigned supreme,
only two alternatives were left for explanation:
either the God of Israel had proved inferior
in battle to the various gods of the Babylonians
and had been completely and utterly vanquished,
or Israel's God had allowed all this
to happen to his people as a punishment.
The thinkers of ancient Israel,
those who struggled to interpret the events
of their history, chose the latter version.

It is difficult for a twentieth-century Christian
to continue to accept such explanations.

The idea that God, the Holy One, whose Son,
the Christ, died to proclaim eternal divine love,
could not only permit but devise and promote
wholesale slaughter, with

   no compassion on young man or virgin, old man or aged,

seems repugnant to most believers today.
We have witnessed in our own generation
the ghastly horrors of global war and holocaust,
the atrocities of the bombing of civilian populations,
the dreadful plight of those who survive
only to languish in refugee camps, and we ask,
If even our human compassion recoils at such scenes,
surely the heart of God cannot accept them,
let alone bring them about.

Teach me, Almighty God, to accept the reality
of your justice, as well as your mercy.
Yet do not permit me ever to accept
the suffering of the innocent.

                       Amen.

2 Chronicles 36:14–23

EVENING

Now in the first year of Cyrus

The problem with rejecting
Old Testament ideas of wholesale divine judgment
is that one must also, to be consistent,
question their equivalent understanding
of God's mercy and redeeming grace.

This story of God's raising up of Cyrus,
king of Persia—an enlightened
yet pagan ruler who sets Israel free,
permits them to return home to Jerusalem,
even to rebuild the temple—has provided
the inspiration for a whole theology of hope.

The joyous prophecies we still love to read
in Second Isaiah, for example,
are based upon this understanding of
God's plan for good King Cyrus.

And unless one can accept a God who punishes,
even if it is only by finally abandoning us
to our own dissolute and despairing ways,
then it is hard to make a case
for the necessity of divine mercy,
the need for God's forgiveness.

The important thing for me is that,
somehow, into all this bewilderment of history
and theology, Jesus the Christ was born,
and that, in some ways at least,
our understanding of his role was shaped
by that of this same Cyrus.

He too came to a captive people
imprisoned in a land far from their home.
He too proclaimed their freedom,
delivered them from the consequences
of their past mistakes and sins,
and set them on the road that would lead
through the wilderness of trial,
back to the kingdom, the true worship
of their God.

In this long wilderness of Lent, Lord God,
inspire me with the vision of the city
that lies up ahead and fit me for the tasks
I must accomplish there in Christ my Lord.

Amen.

DAY THIRTY-TWO

Ephesians 2:4–10

MORNING

But God, who is rich in mercy

It might be argued that
this is the most important "But"
in all theology, in all of human dreaming,
hoping, stretching, scheming, all of human history.

Again and again, the drama of the scriptures
depicts our human plight in its grimmest
yet most honest, realistic terms.
It is a story of continuing rebellion.
It is the story of God's loving quarrel with the world,
of the Lord's continuing campaign to win back
a lost creation to the loving hand
that formed it in the first place.
And at the lowest point of all,
when every human teaching, moral effort,
social program for reform, or revolution,
had been tried and given up on in despair,
we find these words:

But God, who is rich in mercy . . .

and learn about the amazing intervention,
that Love Divine which re-created life—
the broken, twisted thing we had produced for ourselves—
and, having mended it in brokenness upon the cross,
offered it freely back to us renewed in Jesus Christ,
the first life of the new creation.

This pattern fits my personal life as well.
I become so lost, so far wandered from anything
that really is worth living for, so caught up
in every kind of urgent momentary matter,
so impelled, compelled by the sheer motion, the impetus,
momentum of events, that integrity becomes a phantom,
truth a rumor I lost trace of years ago,
and love a bland and vague excuse to cover
my favorite weaknesses.
"But God" does not leave me alone.
And into this bleak vacuum there sounds a voice,
a cry of judgment, a word of invitation to come home.

Let me hear that voice again today, Lord God;
in the quietness and peace of this time of daily prayer,
in the faces of my family, friends, and neighbors,
in the beauty of your world about me,
the stirring of my soul within me, let me know
and claim your grace in Christ my Lord.

Amen.

Ephesians 2:4–10

EVENING

We are his workmanship

This question of good works
has troubled the church from New Testament times
until the present day. The Reformers disputed it.
The popes pronounced concerning it.
And everyday Christians have wondered
ever since just what it is all about.

The problem is not with doing good works.
Just about everyone seems to agree this is desirable.
The problem lies rather with the motivation for
and the expected result of these same good works.
If one performs good works,
the argument runs, in order to please God

and to earn the Lord's favor,
then one is not relying on God's grace alone,
but seeking to earn salvation for oneself.
And this is not the Christian faith.

If, on the other hand,
in total reliance on God's grace
(certainly a praiseworthy position),
one neglects good works completely
and lives a thoroughly selfish life,
trusting completely in the Lord's compassion,
one may well end up theologically blameless
but an absolute failure as a Christian.

This writer to the Ephesians suggests
our good works are nothing we might boast about,
but simply the natural result of the way
that God has re-created us in Christ,
almost as if we were programmed in advance
to live this kind of life.

I find none of these involved and
overrationalized views very helpful.
It seems to me I can perform good works,
try, at least, to live a Christlike life,
and do all this spontaneously, in simple gratitude,
and for the sake of pleasing God, without having
necessarily to intend, presume, or even hope
that I might save my soul by doing so.

Grant me, Lord, the happy privilege of being
a willing and trusting participant in your grace.

Amen.

DAY THIRTY-THREE

Jeremiah 31:31–34

MORNING

Behold, the days are coming, says the LORD

From the very first beginnings,
back when Abram hoped for land to call his own,
a son and heir, according to the promise,
this faith of ours has always had
a leaning to the future.

Firm-rooted in the wisdom and experience
of the past, deeply concerned about God's will
in the here and now, there has always been a promise
up ahead to look forward to; there has always been
a vision to be moved toward in trust.

This new covenant that Jeremiah sang
to exiled Israel centuries before
moves our minds toward the holy week ahead—
and yet behind—recalls us to that upper room,
that sacred meal, that cross-crowned hill
beyond the city wall, the massive rock
that rolled to show the emptiness of the past,
the radiant promise of reality yet to come.

Yet for all the wonder and the terror
of those world-shattering events,
they did not usher in the end,
the fulfillment of every dream and prophecy.
Rather this was itself a new beginning;

reaffirmation, yes, of promises
and covenants of old, and a whole new way
of reaching toward their final consummation.

There still is a promised day
that is to come. Each year as I remember
and retrace the passion of the Lord,
I must not only look back toward his sufferings
and vindication, but also gaze ahead toward
that promised wedding feast
when all will be redeemed,
the original creation is restored
and God's family is reconciled
around one common royal table.

Assist me in these solemn days of preparation, Lord.
May I feel again the almost utter darkness of Golgotha,
yet keep alive that gleam that leads beyond
the garden tomb, into the fullness of eternity.

Amen.

Jeremiah 31:31–34

EVENING

I will put my law within them

I used to read these words
and believe that Jeremiah was
referring to the human conscience,
as if somehow people had evolved since then
from needing to have the laws of God written down
in lawbooks or on great stone tablets
to our current enlightened state, where we can
"let our conscience be our guide."

In fact, of course, the prophet
must have had something else entirely in his mind.
The conscience was a well-developed reality
long before Jeremiah's time; the trouble was

it didn't work any better than it seems to do today.
Knowing God's will, while a complicated matter
much of the time, has never been half as difficult
as actually doing it.

Jeremiah's vision tackles
the harder of these problems.
He foresees a time, promised by the Lord,
when men and women, children too,
will spontaneously do the will of God,
will love and care about each other,
create a just and peaceable society,
and entrust themselves, their ultimate destiny,
into the hands of the only One who can do
anything about it anyway.

All this is far distant from anything
thus far achieved by Judaism, or the church.
And yet the hope is vital for survival.
If love will always be a forced
and grudging thing, indulged in only when
it seems to offer gains to one's own benefit;
if peace can only be, at best, a balance
struck between two mutual terrors,
if justice will remain a partial thing
available only to those who pay the price,
then life is scarcely worth the effort.

Teach me to cherish, Lord,
every free and open impulse toward love,
peace, and justice; and to seize and act
upon them in your name.
                    Amen.

DAY THIRTY-FOUR

Hebrews 5:7–10

MORNING

He learned obedience through what he suffered

Obedience is one of those ideas
which has become devalued in our times.
We have no problem with obedience school for dogs,
and soldiers too need to be trained to obey—
although in today's military we hear more
and more about initiative and creativity.
But simple obedience to orders seems to go
against the grain in this era of rights and liberties.

Some of this is a legacy of this century's atrocities—
all the crimes against humanity perpetrated
by those who were "simply obeying orders."
Yet in many fields of life, in team sports or music,
emergency medical care, the very essence of success
lies in obedience, in willingly subjecting
one's opinions, preferences, impulses to the control
of someone else—a coach, a surgeon, a conductor.

It seems to me that, rather than
throwing out the baby with the bathwater,
we need a more sophisticated understanding
of obedience than we have had before.
We must identify times and circumstances
when obedience is the most appropriate response
and other situations when passive compliance
can spell absolute moral disaster.

The scripture here suggests
that Jesus learned how to obey
through the experience of suffering.
This has also been the testimony of generations
of the saints, that knowing pain of one kind
or another can be an educating influence,
can teach lessons that are available
to be learned in no other way.
We must be careful to avoid masochism here,
but granted the reality and the mystery of pain,
we must not forget that it can be—
has been, for us—miraculously redemptive.

Teach me how to balance my freedom
and my servanthood, Lord God: to use the mind
that you have given me, yet be ready to subject
my will to your holy command. Even if through pain,
teach me Jesus' lesson of true obedience.

Amen.

Hebrews 5:7–10

EVENING

And being made perfect

Once again we are compelled to realize
that the church which produced the New Testament
was not quite sure what to make of Jesus of Nazareth.

One school of thought would seem to suggest
that Jesus was spotless, without fault or imperfection
from the outset, the divine Son of God complete
from Bethlehem to Golgotha, cradle to cross.
Yet this passage from Hebrews, and many others like it,
points to a more gradual process by which the man
Jesus, in a sense, became the Christ,
developed somehow in his relationship to God—
"learned obedience," as the writer puts it here—
until he was "made perfect," "became the source"

of our salvation, and was designated such by God.
Thus we are left with a conflict
between this idea of an imperfect Jesus,
who only gradually grew into his role as Son of God
and Savior, and the traditional view of a sinless Christ
who fully knew his mission from the start.

This whole idea of incarnation,
of God becoming one of us—so central
to our Christian faith—is almost impossible
to comprehend, let alone describe in any detail.
The specific processes by which this miracle
of all miracles took place are simply not available
for human consideration, examination, or analysis.
All we can know, and believe, is that somehow,
in this man Jesus, the Lord of creation revealed himself
and his passionate concern for his wandering people.
In the humanity of Jesus we can see clear
into the divine heart, can glimpse the cosmic pain
of One whose creation turns away in proud rebellion,
can sense the sad but necessary judgment upon all
our weak attempts to save ourselves, can grasp
that vast compassion by which the cross becomes
not humanity's death knell but the key to open up
a new creation for all who will accept its liberation.

As I draw close to you in prayer, Lord Christ,
as I sense your presence here beside me, about me,
even within me, guide my understanding, strengthen faith,
above all deepen my love for you, that I might follow
in the way that you have gone before.
Amen.

DAY THIRTY-FIVE

Psalm 126

MORNING

We were like those who dream

These scriptures are filled with dreamers:
Abram and his dream of beginning a great nation
in the promised land; Joseph, who dreamed dreams
which got him into trouble with his brothers
and yet also served the purposes of God;
Moses, too, who dreamed of liberation
for his captive people; David, for whom
the dream of building God a temple was denied;
and then the prophets who envisioned for God's people
a future time of peace and prosperity
when justice would reign secure
and no one need be afraid.

Jesus, of course, had his dreams;
dreams which he called, "the kingdom of God,"
and which he rooted in the hearts and hopes
of all God's people everywhere.
Peter too, with his vision on the housetop
which led him to a church that knows no barriers;
or Paul, who held on to the yearning vision
that one day Israel, his own people,
would be united with the church of Christ
in one great, universal family of God.
And last of all comes John of Patmos,
who saw through the persecution of his times
to the final triumph of the Lamb,

the glory of the saints, and the coming
of the holy city, New Jerusalem.

Such visionaries these all were;
especially when compared to my own pedestrian hopes:
promotion or a raise in pay, travel, success,
fun, fame and fortune.
Yet there are other dreams I cherish too:
dreams for my family and those I love;
dreams for a better world of peace and harmony,
an end to needless pain, to homelessness and fear;
dreams for my own soul, my restless inner self,
that I might find the holiness I once set out to seek,
that I might know and live the all-embracing joy
I see in Jesus and in the lives
of other Christians.

Lord God, I offer you my dreams; shape them
and shape me around your radiant vision of reality.

Amen.

Psalm 126

EVENING

Then our mouth was filled with laughter

Lent and laughter are not exactly
horse-and-carriage type go-togethers.
This entire season has been seen in the past
as a time for dismal looks and miserable demeanor.
Certainly the contemplation of Christ in his
gallant yet doomed assault upon the ancient walls
of Jerusalem, the city of our pride and prejudice,
must not be made a laughing matter.
There is much in this season
to which the only appropriate response
must be the tears of honest penitence and remorse.

Yet even in this penitential season
joy has its own insistent way of breaking through,
and laughter can never be repressed for long.
That rich old Psalm 100 sings:

Him serve with mirth . . .

and I have always loved it for that suggestion
that our laughter, and not just our tears,
is also a service of God.

This Christian faith of ours
is all too often seen as essentially
a grim and humorless affair, populated by killjoys
who simply cannot bear the dreadful thought
that somewhere someone may be happy.

This is not the view we find of Jesus
in the Gospels. The crowds that flocked to see him,
that sat around his feet to hear his teachings,
that brought their children to him, hoping
that he might lay his hands upon them:
they were not following a pale and dreary masochist.
This was a man who changed water into wine
for a wedding feast—180 gallons of the stuff—
and did it as a sign to show the nature
of his ministry, a man who was accused by
the respectable authorities of being a drunkard
and a clown, so joyful and unrestrained
was the behavior of his disciples.

Restore to me, Lord, the joy of thy salvation.
Let my lips join with the laughter of this whole creation
as we contemplate the glory of your Son
in his redemption of all being.
                              Amen.

DAY THIRTY-SIX

John 12:20–33

MORNING

Sir, we wish to see Jesus

In the pulpit of a church back in Scotland,
my homeland, there is a plaque inscribed with words
which meet the eye of every preacher who stands
in that place. The words are:

   Sir, we would see Jesus.

What a simple request that was
by those Greeks come up to worship in Jerusalem:
a simple request, yet at the same time so profound,
so close to the universal human heart,
that it is echoed to this day in many lands
and countless languages.

The Christian church has much to say to our time
in its preaching, its ministry and mission.
It has a witness to proclaim to every unjust social order,
a word to speak out against bigotry and hate,
a message of peace to present to individuals,
families, communities, and the nations of the world,
a reconciling word of forgiveness and new beginnings
to bear wherever people are divided, set apart
by fear or ancient grudge.
Yet in all of these one constant must remain,
one fundamental factor upon which all else is based,
and that is Jesus Christ, his love, his grace,
his offer of new life bought on the cross.

"Sir, we would see Jesus" is the cry,
not just of congregations hungry for the word
but of starving multitudes who need the bread he broke
and shared so freely. It is the plea of young folk
seeking an ideal, something to live for
in a world of plastic idols, empty dreams,
and of old folk too, who need his gentle, tender hand
to support their failing years.
From prisoners, all kinds of "failures," addicts,
pushers too, prostitutes and politicians, business types,
abusers and abused, that old request comes ringing
down the centuries and reaches us today:

Sir, we would see Jesus.

Grant me, O Lord, the grace to be
at least a partial answer to their cry.
Disclose yourself in me this day.
Thus may I be a channel for your redeeming love.

Amen.

John 12:20–33

EVENING

I . . . will draw all men to myself

What a scene of horror it must have been,
that crucifixion. Three men hung up to die
like raw meat in a butcher's window: their bodies
flogged until the flesh hung in strips,
their blood shed so freely and then congealed
upon the splintered wood and nails, the bitter agony
and torment as they writhed out their final moments
under the merciless sun. This was surely a scene
to be forgotten, a gruesome nightmare to be obliterated,
wiped from human memory as speedily as possible.

And yet it was not so.
The great artists and musicians of our world have,
almost without fail, sought to represent this moment,

to portray the cross in all its terror and wonder.
The writers too, the thinkers, philosophers,
poets, and playwrights have struggled,
almost every one, to express the depth and height,
the dark and light of what took place on Calvary.

Far from being forgotten,
this scene of dread and anguish
with all its rich, unfathomable implications,
has exerted such a fascination,
such a magnetism upon the minds and souls
of humankind, that it can be said to be the crux
of our history, the center from which all things flow,
to which all things must return.

After twenty centuries that magnetism seems,
if anything, more powerful than ever before
as men and women flock to claim the name of Christ
all across the continents of Africa and Asia.
So that the claim, which must have seemed absurd
at the time, the claim of this obscure
carpenter from Nazareth that the cruel death,
which he foresaw, his death upon the cross, would

   draw all men to myself,

this claim has been completely vindicated.
Who was it said the age of miracles is past?

In the quiet of this evening hour,
as I contemplate the tragedy and triumph of your cross,
draw me to yourself, Lord Christ, and claim me,
name me for your own.
                    Amen.

DAY THIRTY-SEVEN

Psalm 51:10–17

MORNING

Create in me a clean heart, O God

One of the most basic prayers ever uttered
is this plea for divine purification.
It comes as the high point of a great song,
the passionate lament of grieving repentance
which is found in Psalm 51.
These are no mere phrases of formal regret,
this is no *pro forma* confession of sins
that the psalmist voices here.
In this beloved psalm,
which has spoken for generation
upon generation of penitent sinners,
the human heart pours forth its bitter disappointment,
its anguish at its own failure to attain
to anything even remotely resembling purity.

Still today, despite all of the pop psychology
which would abolish guilt and repentance as symptoms
of a diseased state of mind, still today the sense of sin
and moral failure plagues the spirit of our times
and cries out for the ancient release of confession,
penitence, and the words of grace, "Go, sin no more."

We have tried to create a perfect race,
the miracles of science, medicine, and technology,
the transforming power of education,
the enlightenment of culture and the arts,

the group ethic of the nation, class, or race,
all these have held out promise for a time
yet have been found profoundly wanting.
It seems that, even at their very best,
education and enlightenment only serve to heighten
the potential both for good and for evil.
The highly educated, enlightened nations of Europe
have demonstrated this in war after murderous war.

This simple prayer,

   Create in me a clean heart, O God,

acknowledges that cleanliness lies far beyond our grasp,
that we cannot hope ever to achieve purity alone,
and then casts the soul on God, the only source
of mercy and of strength to begin anew.

Grant me, by grace, a new beginning, Lord.
Send me forth to this day in the joy of thy salvation
and put a new and right spirit within me.

                            Amen.

Psalm 51:10–17

EVENING

O Lord, open thou my lips

When I open my own lips,
when I seek, by word or deed,
to express myself, assert myself,
to portray or represent myself to others,
the results are all too often horrifying.

If I were able somehow to rewind
and then rerun the utterances of a single day,
I know I would be shocked at the thoughtlessness,
the insensitivity, the pomposity and vanity,
the empty, petty, self-centeredness of it all.
Why is it that my first,

instinctive response is always to defend,
to preserve, to protect my own security,
status, comfort, and well-being?
Why is it that so many of my efforts
appear dedicated to convincing others—
and thus, perhaps, myself—
that I am really worthy of attention,
someone of stature and importance,
someone superior to the general run
of members of this human race?

When God opens my lips,
as happens in odd, miraculous moments,
I find myself not claiming or complaining,
not asserting or attacking, not belittling
or deceiving, or concealing, but singing.

When God opens my lips
I sing a song that is not aria,
not solo, but a chorus in which I blend
my own unique melody into the one majestic harmony
that rings through all creation.

When God opens my lips
I know a joy that flows from deep within
to meet a fuller, richer joy without.
I sense a laughter which pervades all being,
not denying pain but moving through
and then beyond it into ecstasies
that have not yet been imagined,
let alone set down.

    Lord, open thou my lips.

Amen.

DAY THIRTY-EIGHT

Philippians 3:8–14

MORNING

I count everything as loss

This kind of all-or-nothing talk
that Paul expresses here reminds me
of the logic and the poetry of love songs,
where life without the beloved
is simply not worth living.

Yet there ought not to be too much surprise
in that observation. Paul's devotion to his Lord,
his passionate commitment to the One
who set him free from his previous obsession
with the law and its impossible demands,
had much in common with the kind of bond
that forms between two lovers.

Christ's love for Paul was so powerful,
so demanding, that it dazzled him into blindness
and literally knocked him to the ground.
From that time forward,
after he recovered his sight,
Paul never saw things in the same way again.
It was as if his eyes remained fixed upon Christ;
and everything he saw, he saw within the outline of
and lighted by the radiance of his risen Lord.

From this new perspective, everything else
in all creation became of secondary importance,

drew its validity, even its reality, from
the one overwhelming fact of God's redeeming love
in Jesus Christ. For Paul every experience—
success or shipwreck, friendship or flogging,
preaching or prison—was to be evaluated
not by its effect upon himself,
but by its value, its usefulness
to the gospel of his Lord.

Such single-minded devotion frightens me, Lord God.
My own days are filled with passionate attachments
to all sorts of persons and things: my spouse
and children, my job, my home, my newest
or next car, my garden, or my health.
I fear to compare these with my love for Christ
because I am pretty sure what the answer would be.
Dazzle me with your love, O Christ,
drive me to my knees, that I might rise
to love all things as I rediscover them in you.

Amen.

Philippians 3:8–14

EVENING

That I may know him

It is a common wish on the part of Christians
to have actually known the Lord,
to have walked the roads of Galilee beside him,
to have been present when he healed the sick,
fed the hungry, and taught the multitudes.
"If only I had known him," people say,
"it would have been so much easier to believe."

It comes as a surprise, at times, to realize
that Paul—probably Jesus' greatest interpreter—
never actually knew the Lord Jesus either;
that, just like Christians today, Paul was not present
when the great adventure of our faith began.

Yet the apostle talks and writes as if he knew Christ;
and here in this passage he gives a clue as to how
this might be possible both for him, and also
for believers of all ages.

That I may know him and the power of his resurrection,
and may share his sufferings, becoming like him in his death.

Paul is telling me here that if I entrust my life
and death into Christ's hands, if I am willing
to endure suffering for the sake of others,
just as he did, if I am willing to share the fate
he met for our sakes upon the cross,
then I can know the Lord, even as Paul did;
then the Lord will walk beside me in the way.

This seems a lot to ask.
There are so many "ifs" in this promise
Paul proposes, so many conditions to be fulfilled,
and I am not at all sure I can meet the requirements
there for knowing Christ the Lord.
I may be willing to make an occasional sacrifice
for others' sake, to bear a certain amount of suffering
once in a while, but, to be completely honest,
going all the way to the cross with him is far beyond
anything I am capable of right now.

Lord Christ, forgive my lack of faith,
my failure to live up to the standards set forth
in this passage by the apostle Paul,
and grant me in this evening hour of prayer
to know the sureness of your presence,
the power of your resurrection.
                              Amen.

DAY THIRTY-NINE

Isaiah 43:16–21

MORNING

Thus says the LORD

They said it with such assurance,
these prophets of the olden times in Israel,
sounded it forth as preface to their message—

Thus says the LORD—

and the people trembled.

Preachers don't use this phrase much anymore.
They tend to say "It seems to me" or
"On the whole I tend to agree with. . . ."
Oh, a few still use the words—I see them on TV—
but from what they then go on to say,
the Lord's chief concern is helping them raise money
for their latest project, crisis of the month.

It seems things are more complicated
than they used to be in the prophets' time;
and simple clear-cut answers of right and wrong,
good and evil, are almost impossible to come by.
Perhaps we know more than they did, see more fully
with the aid of our sophisticated media, libraries,
and computers the entire picture, with all
its ramifications and interconnections.
But then again, maybe they knew more than we do.
Is it that the Lord of hosts is speaking
less distinctly than in days gone by?

Or are we merely listening less carefully,
less faithfully?

Some things, at least, are just as simple
and clear-cut as they ever were. The same God,

> who makes a way in the sea,
> a path in the mighty waters,

is still a liberating Lord,
hating all forms of oppression and captivity,
seeking to eliminate injustice, poverty,
hunger, and disease from the world.
This Lord despises all hypocrisy,
everything that is false, untrue, that seeks
to deceive, to seduce or live a lie.
While I may not say, "Thus says the Lord,"
surely I can take my stand on basic truths like these.

Guide me, Lord, where it is possible,
to cut through the complexity of issues of my time
and to act upon them honestly and courageously
in the light of your clear, shining word.

Amen.

Isaiah 43:16–21

EVENING

Remember not the former things

This is not exactly
what I would expect to read
in the pages of the Bible.
My experience of this old book is that
it is continually calling upon people to remember,
that again and again the cry goes out to recall
the blessings of the Lord, the great deliverances
of the past, and then, on that very basis,
to act with confidence in the present
and for the future.

Memory seems to play a key function
in the processes of faith, both for Jew
and for Christian—the peoples of the Bible.
At the very heart of the central rite of Judaism,
the Passover celebration, the Jew is called upon
to remember he or she was once Pharaoh's slave in Egypt
and that the Lord has wrought deliverance with
mighty hand and outstretched arm.
While at the core of the Lord's Supper
there is repeated the command of Jesus to

do this in remembrance of me.

Why, then, does Isaiah here call upon the people
to forget the past and look toward the future?
Specifically for this prophet, he believed
that Israel had focused long enough on the mistakes
of yesterday and that the Lord was about to inaugurate
a completely new age with the return of the exiles
from captivity in Babylon.

And countless times since then,
in the life of the church and of individual believers,
the moment has arrived when the focus has to shift
from what the Lord has done to what the Lord is doing,
from the glories that have been to the challenge
of the present, the promise of the future.
Memory is absolutely vital to the faith,
but never in and of itself, always as a foundation
for faithful action in the here and now.

Teach me, great Lord of time and of eternity,
when to remember and when to forget. Ground my faith
in the history of your steadfast love and mercy.
Yet fit me for discipleship now.
                              Amen.

PALM SUNDAY

Matthew 21:1–11

MORNING

All the city was stirred, saying, "Who is this?"

They didn't even know yet;
after all the months of ministry,
teaching and healing, working miracles,
living out in words and deeds and attitudes
God's judgment and God's grace, they didn't even know yet.

That procession into the city,
that jubilant yet ironic scene of triumph—
laughable in the eyes of the world,
the Roman conquerors, the power structures of that day
and every day since then—that parade with palms
for banners, ragged cast-off garments for a royal carpet,
led by a king upon a donkey, was a dead giveaway,
should have been obvious if they had known
their prophets, their Zechariah and his glad cry
to the daughters of Jerusalem.

> Lo, your king comes to you;
> triumphant and victorious is he,
> humble and riding on an ass,
> on a colt the foal of an ass.

Yet still they asked, "Who is this?"

We still ask, "Who is this?"
as if we had not seen the signs, had not read
the prophets, as if two thousand years of proof,

of evidence made visible in human lives,
had never been recorded.
The great leaders of his day,
high priests and governors, even Caesars,
world figures whose names were at the tip of
every tongue on that festival day in old Jerusalem,
are now long forgotten; their faded memory lies
in the dust, while his grows ever stronger,
means salvation, brings life to millions
wherever it is preached.

How can we not know, after all this?
How can I not recognize my King, my Lord,
my Savior in this scene of humble majesty
combined with divine love?

Draw me to your side this Holy Week,
Lord Christ. Let me participate in all its moments,
the trials as well as the triumphs.
Thus may I learn again just who you are,
and who you are calling me to be.

Amen.

Luke 19:28–44

EVENING

The very stones would cry out

Was he speaking metaphorically here?
Surely Jesus did not literally mean that
if he were to command his exuberant followers
to be silent, the rocks and pebbles by the roadside
would break out into a song of praise.
Or did he?

Certainly for one who had worked
the nature miracles of walking on the waters
and stilling the stormy sea of Galilee
this could not be called a clear impossibility.

Certainly, too, the Hebrew scriptures—
Jesus' own sacred writings—
when they portray the coming of the Lord,
the salvation of our God, are filled
with similar images of laughing mountains,
singing fields, and trees that clap their hands.
Indeed, this statement to the Pharisees
could have been yet another sign,
another chance for them to realize that
the kingdom was upon them,
that the long-expected Day of God
was actually dawning in their midst,
before their eyes and ears.

There are passages also in the New Testament
which would support a similar concept.
Paul writes in Romans that the whole creation,
the entire cosmos, is somehow yearning,
eagerly awaiting the revelation of God's children,
the liberation and restoration of everything
that exists to its original created glory.
The great climax of the book of Revelation
depicts a new heaven and new earth in which
the holy city, like an enormous radiant jewel,
descends to earth from God.
So that it seems as if not only humankind
but the entire created universe participates
in some basic all-embracing fashion
in the redemption that Christ brings.

Grant me the humility, Lord, to see my place
as part of an entire creation trusting in your grace.
Then let me play my part and bear your grace
to everyone and everything that needs it.

Amen.

DAY FORTY-ONE

Isaiah 42:1–9

MORNING

Behold my servant

So this is what it means
to be the chosen one of the Lord,
to be one in whom the soul of God delights.
Not much privilege here, or status, or prestige.
There seems to be no mention of priority ranking,
of a first claim to special places in the kingdom.
The emphasis instead is on a job that must be done,
a service to be performed. And the title
one receives is that of Servant:

> Behold my servant, whom I uphold,
> my chosen, in whom my soul delights.

This is the way it goes, in fact,
all through the history of God's people.
Their great leaders—men like Moses, Samuel,
even David—know little of the glory and the pomp
of the high offices they hold. For the most part
their lives are spent—worn out—in service
of the God who chose them to be servants.

The people too, "the chosen race,"
as they have been called, God's own elect,
began as slaves in Egypt.
And even though God led them out to freedom,
their history, with brief exceptions,
is one long tale of testing, trial, and failure,

of conflict and captivity.
To be chosen, for the Jews,
was a privilege that many of them
might just as readily have done without,
in exchange for a little peace and dull prosperity.

As this Holy Week moves on,
Jesus too discovers, more and more,
the dimensions and requirements that accompany
and define his unique destiny of chosenness.
The service he is called upon to offer,
not just to God but on behalf of our entire
human race, looms ever larger as the days go by.
He sees the way, the gentle and nonviolent way,
in which he is to "bring forth justice."

As I try to follow in his footsteps, Lord,
show me the power in his gentleness,
the world-transforming strength he found in service.

Amen.

Isaiah 42:1–9

EVENING

He will bring forth justice

If there is one thing,
one quality of life, one gift above all others
that these Hebrew people sought from God,
it appears to have been justice.

More than the love of God,
so stressed in the New Testament,
even more than the mercy of God, which is
emphasized by Jews and Christians alike,
these people of the covenant desired
to receive justice from their Lord.

Could it be that honest justice
was such a rarity in those earlier times,
and crooked judges and twisted laws had become
so commonplace, that the only hope they had
of a fair trial was to seek one from the Lord?
Or was it rather that justice meant for them
far more than any system of laws and courts,
judges and prisons and such?

In fact justice, as the prophets saw it,
encompassed the whole nation and its way of life.
True justice, of the kind that Israel's God
will someday bring about, will abolish all inequity,
will do away with poverty, hunger, and want,
oppression and intimidation too, and will provide
a social order in which all people will sit under
their own vine and their own fig tree,
and none shall make them afraid.

As Jesus moved about the streets,
the busy gathering places of Jerusalem
during Holy Week, showing no fear
for the authorities, answering their tricky,
treacherous questions with courage and clear honesty,
he was establishing justice; he was going about
the work Isaiah had set forth so long before,
the work of the servant of the Lord.

Let me share this view of justice, Lord.
As I see my neighbors in the turmoil and the trouble
of our cities, teach me to be concerned not just
for crime but for your justice, for a society
based on justice and on liberty for all.

Amen.

DAY FORTY-TWO

2 Corinthians 1:8–22

MORNING

In him it is always yes

This text might give the impression
that there can be no negative in Christ,
that there is no such thing as a No
in the vocabulary of our Lord.

> For the Son of God, Jesus Christ . . .
> was not Yes and No;
> but in him it is always Yes,

writes Paul, in answering his critics
in the church at Corinth. This expression
could be seen as extremely permissive.

If it is really "always Yes" with Christ,
does that imply that everything is permitted,
that it doesn't matter what I do or think, believe
or say, because the grace of God in Jesus
will make everything OK? But this would make
a mockery of any kind of ethics or moral code.
And Paul, in the epistle to the Romans,
has already argued against such an interpretation
of God's free grace, suggesting that,
while we cannot be saved by the power of the law,
we are still under its tutelage, its guidance,
to teach us how to live the Christian life.

It seems to me that Paul is writing here
less about the negatives of faith and more
about equivocation, about talking out of both sides
of one's mouth at once. To certain Corinthians
who have accused Paul of being unreliable,
or, perhaps, indecisive, he reminds them
that there was nothing indecisive about the gospel
he had preached to them, and that the Lord
he preached about was anything but unreliable.

All the promises of God find their Yes in him,

Paul goes on to say: thus claiming that whatever
had been written or proclaimed in the past
concerning God was now fulfilled,
had been fully proved to be completely reliable
in the life and death and resurrection
of Jesus Christ, the Son of God.

Let me live this day in the confidence
that comes from your eternal Yes, good Lord.
But may I also listen for the No that guards me
from the ways of shame and death.
                                        Amen.

2 Corinthians 1:8–22

EVENING

That is why we utter the Amen through him

I used to wonder why we always
close our prayers with the words,
"Through Jesus Christ our Lord. Amen."
In this tight-packed little passage
I discover that this phrase from Paul
has been the customary usage of the Christian church
at prayer from its very earliest days.

But more than this I learn that these words
are not merely a ritual conclusion, a holy formula
we can add on at the end of our requests,

like some pious seal of approval.
Paul's reasoning here suggests that this phrase,
"Amen—So be it," can be said with utter confidence
by Christians, and not just as an expression
of longing and fervent hope.

Through Jesus Christ our Lord we have
far more than hope; we have the assurance
from his lips that our prayers are heard and answered
Through Jesus Christ our Lord we know that a God
whose only Son was sent to live with us
and offer up his life for our sakes
will surely stand by any and all promises:

    For all the promises of God find their Yes in him.

Through Jesus Christ our Lord we can be certain
that our God will stop at nothing to win back
his lost and wandering people, will pursue us,
in undying love, through rejection, death, and hell,
if need be, until at last we yield and turn
from fear, frustration, and futility toward
the light we were created for, the life
that feeds our hungry souls forever.

Through Jesus Christ our Lord we trust
this God will surely grant the wishes and desires
of our hearts in such a way—not necessarily the way
we ask them—but in such a way as leads us
to accept his grace, his mercy, and his life
for us, in us, and for his kingdom.

Through Jesus Christ my Lord I pray tonight,
secure in knowing that your peace, great God,
will hold me safe until the morning light.

                                             Amen.

DAY FORTY-THREE

Jeremiah 15:15–21

MORNING

Like a deceitful brook . . . ?

I remember reading somewhere
that in the original Hebrew text
there is no question mark at this point.
In fact, some of the newer translations
of the scriptures reflect this later insight,
so that Jeremiah does not ask *whether* the Lord
is like a deceitful brook that dries up;
rather, he accuses the Lord of being to him
just like a treacherous stream which is
transformed into a dry riverbed
in the very moment of his need.

I suspect the reason this lesson
is selected for this day in Holy Week
is to lead me to reflect upon the premonitions,
doubts, and fears which—despite his faith in God—
must have been tormenting the mind of Jesus
in these days of turmoil and dispute.
He surely knew about the plots
that were being hatched around him.
By his own words at the last supper we learn
that Judas' bargain with the rulers of the temple
was known about by Jesus in advance.
And in the garden of Gethsemane—that place where,
even today, the ancient olive trees distill
a sense of anguish from the air—

in Gethsemane we know that Jesus poured
the heartache of his spirit out in prayer
that, if possible, he might be spared the trial
he seemed about to undergo.

It is important to me that such persons,
the prophet Jeremiah, and even Christ himself,
could know fear, perhaps even doubt the faithfulness
of the Lord. Jeremiah's angry cry that God has deceived him
rings true to my own life at times: those times when
all appears lost, no future ahead worth thinking of,
and prayer, any prayer that I can mumble out,
is failing to rise above the level
of my own bootstraps.

Be with me even in my anger, Lord,
especially when I feel betrayed, and remind me
of the path that your Son trod on my behalf;
let me feel his companionship in the way.

Amen.

Jeremiah 15:15–21

EVENING

Thy words became to me a joy

The prophet here, in a time of anguish,
remembers the earlier days of his ministry
and looks back on them with longing,
wishing for their return.
He looks back in puzzlement,
as suffering Job must also have done:
trying to see where he went wrong,
remembering the eagerness with which he had set out,
asking the Lord just where it was he fell short
in the mission God had given him.

Like so many believers, even today,
Jeremiah seeks to explain current unhappiness,

suffering, and misfortune in terms of divine punishment
for some past, unperceived failure on his part.

> Why is my pain unceasing,
>> my wound incurable,
>> refusing to be healed?

This is a cry most human beings will cry
at one time or another. It foreshadows
that great cry, the cry of desolation on the cross,

> My God, my God, why hast thou forsaken me?

The reply of God, when it comes,
offers no real answer to the aggrieved plea,
"What did I do wrong?"
The Lord does not descend
to the level of swapping accusations
with his servant, of justifying, in any way,
the mysteries of pain and human suffering.

Instead God offers Jeremiah a promise,
a commitment and a guarantee that whatever
anguish he might have to undergo, he will survive—

> they will fight against you,
> but they shall not prevail over you—

and then adds to this that word
which also came to Moses, David, all those
troubled shapers of the faith in other ages:

> I will deliver you.

Such words must have been very close
to Jesus' heart and soul throughout these days
of gathering storm clouds in Jerusalem.
Inscribe them, too, on my soul, Lord,
that in my hour of testing I hold firm
to you, as you hold firm to me.
Amen.

MAUNDY THURSDAY

Mark 14:12–26

MORNING

Take; this is my body

So many times these holy words
have been repeated down the centuries,
and in so many different places, corners
of the globe, so many circumstances—
from palaces to prison cells—
so many meanings, strengths, and promises
found within their simple depth.

One might add, of course,
so many disputes, divisions,
battles, even, fought over the precise
definition of these six small syllables,
so many nations, communities, even families
torn apart in the attempt to impose
one interpretation above all the rest.

Whatever the fine points of their theology,
there lies within these words a simpler meaning
upon which, one would hope, all Christians
might someday come together and agree.
When we eat bread, in just this way,
recalling Christ and all he did for us,
he is present to us, really present—
although precisely how remains a mystery.

Not only is he present,
but, as the bread is broken, shared,
consumed within the remembering community,
the living Christ will enter faithful hearts
and lives and give them his own strength,
bring grace and nourishment for the soul,
new life to all who seek it in his name;
more than this, will bind together those who eat
in a fellowship of love and service,
a family which reaches out to join
with other families across the globe
and build a world of lasting peace, true justice.

As I remember today how Jesus instituted
this family meal, Lord God, may the bread of life—
his life—revive my faltering spirit, set me firm
within that company who go singing forth to face
the darkness and distrust, the sad betrayals
of this world, and look with him beyond,
toward the promised dawn of Easter Day.

Amen.

1 Corinthians 11:23–29

EVENING

This cup is the new covenant in my blood

Reaching, once again,
behind the learned debates
concerning the exact meaning of
the symbols invoked here—setting aside,
for the moment, the many involved questions
about just how the spilling of Christ's blood
could bring about a new covenant, a fresh,
restored relationship between God and humankind—
I catch the sudden image of a thorn-ripped brow,
nail-punctured hands and feet; I shudder as I see
in my mind's eye, the bitten lip, clenched teeth,
and horror-widened eyes of my Savior, who

in unrelenting love poured out his
life's blood for my sake.

`This graceful sacrament we celebrate,
so calm and lovely in its words and gestures,
even the linens and the artifacts we bring to deck
the holy table: all these display our joy
and gratitude for what was done.
Yet amid all this beauty I sometimes feel
we fail to sense the fear, to feel the terror
that has to be involved here also.
This feast is about bloodshed,
and before we rush to taste the wonder,
sing the triumph of it all, do we not need
to calculate again the cost, the price he paid
to seat us round this table; should we not realize
anew our part in making all this necessary?

On this Maundy Thursday night—
with its sad litanies of treachery,
conspiracy, deceit, and cowardice; the dark
and evil shadows that gather ever closer round
the truest and most generous life that ever lived;
that searing, lonely hour of anguish in the garden
lost among the olive trees—can I not watch and wait
with him one hour tonight to share his agony?

Lay heavy on my heart this night,
Lord God, the suffering of your abandoned son.
Wind deep into the sinews of my faith
the aching loneliness he must have known for me.
And make me worthy, by his grace, to share
his task, to heal this broken world.
                                    Amen.

GOOD FRIDAY

Luke 23:32–56

MORNING

Today you will be with me in Paradise

Why do we call this Friday "good,"
when everything we did in it was bad?
Why do we call this week "holy,"
when everything that happened in it
seems to have been so unholy,
so corrupted with the worst of human
cruelty, selfishness, and fear?
Why do we remember this time each year,
this day when we took everything that was good,
that was God-with-us in the world,
and rejected it, got rid of it, did away with it,
nailing it up on a tree to die?

And yet this day did have its moments,
one might even say its saving moments.
There were, after all, those faithful women
standing their witness by the cross,
courageous, true, and caring to the end
and beyond the end.

There was the thief who,
of all the people gathered there,
recognized his sovereign Lord in his
most lordly act, the act of conquering death.
There was the Roman soldier who, however dimly,

could not help perceive the undefeated glory
in the man that he had put to death.

And Joseph too—a Joseph
at the end as there was at the beginning—
Joseph of Arimathea, a man of influence
and secret faith who at the last,
at least, could use that influence
to find his Lord a resting place.

Even so, Lord, may I too
be privileged to be among those witnesses
beside the cross this day of evil and of good.
In the quiet, somber midday hours of worship,
or even as I go about my daily tasks,
teach me to wait and watch in sorrow and in joy.
Help me, above all, to place my life, my soul,
my destiny as they did, in his broken,
healing hands, that in his mercy
I may be with him in Paradise.

Amen.

John 19:17–42

EVENING

It is finished

What was it that was finished that dread day
on Calvary's hill? What exactly was completed,
as Jesus gave this final rending cry?
Did he mean, perhaps, his cause was finished,
his plan to save the world brought to a brutal close?
Might he have been referring to the end
of his own torment, that long, slow process,
bleeding, gasping, choking, yielding at the last
to pain that tore him limb from limb?

Might Jesus have meant suffering was ended,
that henceforth those who believe in him
will no longer have to undergo pain?

But suffering continues still; each day transports
its load of crucifixions: young folk struck down
by disease and violence, parents ripped from
their stunned families by random accident,
babies come to birth only to die before
they ever hear the tender words of mother love.

Might he have meant that sin is finished,
the power of evil broken by the cross?
Yet twenty centuries on, these powers are still
a lively, prospering presence in the world:
from the poisons of pollution to the tragedy
of starvation, from the moral death of corruption
and injustice to the literal death that lies
in stockpiles ready to be unleashed.

What, then, was it that was finished by this death?
Surely it was the separation, that gulf, begun
at Eden's tree, dividing God from his rebellious children:
all those aching centuries of blind rejection
holding God at bay. All this was ended
when God came and lived among us,
accepted our rejection, even to the cruel point
of death upon the cross, and stretching out his arms
bridged the yawning gap of guilt with his own love.

For all that ended, Lord, all that began
on this Good Friday, I thank you now and offer you
myself. Let my living also form a bridge
to those who still deny your grace,
to all who walk in darkness yearning for
a gleam of hope, a word of peace.

                                        Amen.

HOLY SATURDAY

Ezekiel 37:1–14

MORNING

Can these bones live?

Surely this was
the most desolate day of all.
The Savior had been killed and laid in the tomb.
The hope of the world, despised and rejected,
was cast out of the world as if to say,
"Take back your son, your Word made flesh,
your love set down among us. He is too good for us.
His judgment worries us. His mercy threatens us.
He wants us to change, to be better than we are,
to be the fully alive persons you created us to be,
and that is too much work, too much to ask.
With every word he speaks, every breath he breathes,
he challenges our comfortable, shallow existence;
and if we permit him to go on much longer, who knows
what he might love us into doing, into being?
Here he is, Lord; he is all yours.
Take him back now, and leave us alone.
We would rather have it that way."

And so it could have ended.
In fact, so it did end, still does end,
for most of God's children, most of the time.
We live, we still exist, most of us,
in a Holy Saturday world: a world
where a cold Christ lies buried in the tomb
and life goes on its not-so-merry way,

honoring his teachings in the breach,
acknowledging his memory once or twice a year,
and getting along very nicely still without him,
"Thank you very much!"

Yet what do we do for hope,
for vision and promise for the future?
The next vacation, next promotion, next new car
eventually lose all their allure as the years go by
and time grows shorter. What do we do for forgiveness
as the casualty toll of living mounts and our days
are shaped more by the past's mistakes
than by the possibilities ahead?

Lord God, this Holy Saturday
I see my own life in the grave, bound tight
within the bands of habit, apathy, and fear.
Can these bones live? I wait your word
of resurrection and of life.

Amen.

Ezekiel 37:1–14

EVENING

And I will bring you home

This intervening day stands trembling
on the threshold between bloodshed and birth.
Was it merely a waiting period, necessary to fulfill
the prophecies of old, or was some cosmic struggle
taking place: the decisive battle of life
against death, resurrection versus oblivion?

Ezekiel's dramatic vision of the valley of dry bones
tells of a God who brings his people home,
who seeks out the exiled and the lost—
the living dead—and returns them to their own land,
to the place where they belong.

> Behold, I will open your graves, and raise you
> from your graves . . . and I will bring you home.

One of the fascinating speculations,
seen as early as the first epistle of Peter,
is that during this interim time between cross
and empty tomb Jesus went and preached his gospel
to "the spirits in prison"; in other words, to those
who were in hell and had never heard the good news
of redemption. Jesus went and called them home,
extended, in that grim and awful setting,
the loving invitation of the father to the prodigal:
"Come home, my child. I miss you.
We need each other. Let's begin again."

There is a calling home within this shadowed day,
an invitation to return, to rest beneath
the wings of the Almighty and to wait
in humble, quiet, trusting faith
for the salvation of our God to be revealed.

This idea of "home," this dream of a "homecoming,"
lies deep within each one of us, informs our yearnings,
motivates our reaching toward light and meaning.
The promise that lies waiting to be born,
to be fulfilled, throughout this day
is that the door is flung wide open,
the welcome mat is out, and God waits
with open arms for our arrival.

Hold me within your arms this night, O God,
and bring me in the morning to the empty tomb,
the open door, the way home to life eternal.

Amen.

EASTER DAY

Matthew 28:1–10

MORNING

And rolled back the stone

A piece of the rock,
that's what people want nowadays—
something solid and dependable that
will stand the tests of time; in other words,
security, protection guaranteed, nailed down,
sealed tight, foolproof against the triple threat
of suffering, tragedy, and failure. We build lives
around such goals, spend our days pursuing education,
real estate, investments, precious metals, locks
and chains, alarms for every window, every door.
And all this to protect ourselves
in a chancy, risky world.

Yet the more secure people get,
the more afraid they become;
the more layers of protection they amass,
the more they dread the loss of those defenses.
Until, just like that massive rock on Jesus' tomb,
the "piece of the rock" they sought after
seals them off from life, from freedom, and from love.
So it is that, long before death actually claims us,
we crawl inside our cozy air-conditioned tombs
and seal the entrance shut.

This day is one for rolling stones away.
This day is one for realizing, admitting to ourselves

that for all our stocks and bonds, for all our power,
prestige, property, prosperity, we can never,
never make ourselves ultimately secure.
We carry conscience with us behind all protective walls;
that and the consciousness that, soon or late,
the hour will come when we will be no more.

Roll away my heavy rock, O risen Christ.
Tear down all the defenses I have built around
my anxious self. Let your resurrected glory sweep away
like chaff the empty, false securities I cling to,
and set me kneeling at your feet, knowing again
the one thing that can conquer fear is love,
the one gift that can lead to life is life,
life seized and lived out to the full
in bold and daring freedom.
Roll away my rock, Lord; raise me
with soaring alleluias from my fearful death
to everlasting life in you.

Amen.

Luke 24:13–35

EVENING

What had happened on the road

This tale of the Emmaus road
is a fascinating one for Christians
in this present day and age.
It speaks to our condition in our active,
traveling, mobile way of life that the risen Christ
revealed himself in the course of a journey.

Mary in the garden is a poetic scene,
with much about it full of grace and beauty.
But I tend to see it from afar, like a lovely
medieval masterpiece in an art gallery.
These two travelers, on the other hand,
making their sad, dejected way out of the city

where their hopes and dreams had been destroyed,
pouring out the burden of their broken hearts
to that sympathetic stranger on the way:
I read their tale and feel I walk beside them.

As he explains to them the hidden,
glorious meaning of the events they have seen,
my heavy heart grows lighter,
my mind begins to wonder and perceive.
And when they ask him to abide with them,
invite him in to share a simple evening meal,
a sense of blessing kindles in my soul.

That moment when he takes the bread
and tears it in that certain way, just so,
can bring the tears to my eyes even now,
across so many centuries. And then I hasten
with them back the way they came; yes, back
to dread, bloodstained Jerusalem with all its menace
and alarm, to bear the news, the greatest news
that ever came to pass:
The Lord is risen!
He is risen indeed!

Walk beside me, living Lord,
down all the roads that lie ahead.
When I am puzzled and perplexed, when I doubt
myself or, even worse, doubt you, draw close
and make things clearer to my sight.
And when I reach that final evening's rest,
abide with me, reveal to me your own self
in the breaking of the bread.
Amen.